# THE ONLY CRYPTOCURRENCY INVESTING BOOK YOU'LL EVER NEED

AN ABSOLUTE BEGINNER'S GUIDE TO THE BIGGEST "MILLIONAIRE MAKER" ASSET OF 2022 AND BEYOND—INCLUDING HOW TO MAKE MONEY FROM NFTS

FREEMAN PUBLICATIONS

# TOP 3 CRYPTOS TO BUY NOW (APRIL 2022 UPDATE)

Each one of these has minimum 50x potential upside and all 3 have catalyst events in the next month poised to spur significant growth.

**Coin 1:** Dubbed "The Ethereum Killer" - this coin boasts the world's fastest blockchain which can process transactions 2000x faster than Ethereum at a fraction of the cost

**Coin 2:** The fastest growing blockchain gaming protocol in the world (and unlike other gaming projects - this is NOT just a single game)

**Coin 3:** The "Blockchain of Blockchains" which facilitates interoperability between different coins and solves the biggest problem in crypto right now: scalability

Get your free copy of this report by going to
https://freemanpublications.com/top3

Or text the word **BONUS** to 844-968-4152 (US only)

# BONUSES

All of these bonuses are 100% free, with no strings attached. You don't need to enter any details except your email address.

https://freemanpublications.com/bonus

Or text the word BONUS to 844-968-4152 (US only)

**Free bonus #1: Company Valuation 101 video course ($97 value)**

In this 8 part video course, you'll discover our process for accurately valuing a company. This will help you determine if a stock is overvalued, correctly valued, or a bargain. Giving you an indicator of whether to buy or not.

**Free bonus #2: Guru Portfolios Analyzed ($37 value)**

In these videos, we analyze the stock portfolios of Billionaire investors like Warren Buffett. As well as top entrepreneurs like Bill Gates.

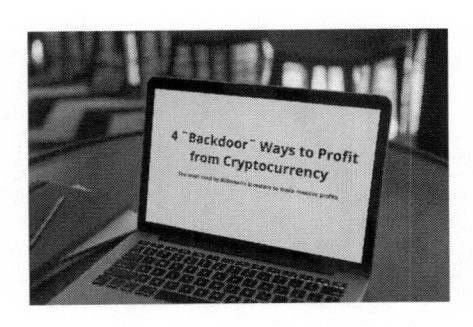

**Free bonus #3: 4 "Backdoor" Ways to Profit from Cryptocurrency ($47 value)**

When you have a paradigm-shifting technology like cryptocurrency and blockchain ... there are multiple ways to profit from it.

But before you rush out and buy every altcoin under the sun... there is a smarter way of doing this.

The ways used by hedge funds and Billionaire investors to make massive profits from the price of Bitcoin and other cryptocurrencies.

And you don't need anything more than a regular brokerage account to do so.

We covered exactly how to do this in a private call for our premium members recently and you´ll get access to this video for free.

**Free bonus #4: 2 Stocks to Sell Right Now ($17 value)**

These 2 stocks are in danger of plummeting in the next 12 months. They're both popular with retail investors, and one is even in the top 5 most held stocks on Robinhood. Believe us; you don't want to be holding these going into 2021 and beyond.

**Free bonus #5: AI Disruptor - The $4 Stock Poised to be the Next Big Thing in Computing ($17 value)**

This under the radar company, which less than 1% of investors have heard of, is at the forefront of a breakthrough technology that will change our lives as we know them. Soon this technology will be in every smartphone, tablet, and laptop on the planet.

### Free bonus #6: Options 101 ($17 Value)

Options don't have to be risky. In fact, they were invented to *reduce* risk. It's no wonder that smart investors like Warren Buffett regularly use options to supplement their long-term portfolio. In this quick start guide, we show you how options work and why they are tools to be utilized rather than feared.

### Free bonus #7: The 1 Dividend Stock to Buy and Hold for the Rest of Your Life ($17 Value)

Dividends are the lifeblood of any income investor, and this stock is a cornerstone of any dividend strategy. A true dividend aristocrat with consistent payouts for over 50 years which you'll want to add to your portfolio for sure.

### Free bonus #8: All the images inside this book in color ($17 Value)

As much as we'd like to print these books in full color, the printing costs prohibit us from doing so. So on our website, you can get all the images from the book in full color.

All of these bonuses are 100% free, with no strings attached. You don't need to enter any details except your email address.

https://freemanpublications.com/bonus

# INTRODUCTION: THE STATE OF THE CRYPTOCURRENCY MARKET IN 2022

Not a day goes by where I don't receive an email from readers asking me about my thoughts on the cryptocurrency market. Our wheelhouse has always been stock market investing, and even with the release of our bestselling Bitcoin book last year, that hasn't quenched the market's thirst for well reasoned, rational information about cryptocurrency.

For good reason, new asset classes don't come around often. If you think of the 4 most common asset classes that individual investors own (stocks, bonds, gold and real estate), all of these have existed for more than 100 years, with gold and real estate going back thousands of years. Sure, we've seen derivatives of these like ETFs, options and REITs, but never a brand new asset class like cryptocurrency. At least not in my lifetime.

What has existed in my lifetime is financial fads. We had the dotcom boom in the late 90s, followed by the global financial crisis in 2008, and more recently, the rise of cryptocurrency.

Which leads us to the question, where does crypto fall on the spectrum? Is it a life changing asset class or a financial fad? The correct answer is, both. More people than ever before will become millionaires because of cryptocurrency, but many ordinary investors will get burned and lose their shirts. My aim with this book is to ensure that you're in the first category.

Let's ground ourselves with some numbers. The total cryptocurrency market value has ballooned from $145 billion in 2017 to over $2.5 trillion by the middle of 2021 (Kharpal, 2021). This means around a 15-fold increase in just over 4 years.

Meaning that if you had invested $10,000 in Bitcoin and Ethereum in 2017, your investment value as of October 2021 would have increased to more than $270,000. Mind you, I mentioned only the two largest cryptocurrencies and not some obscure ones. Our own recommendation to buy Bitcoin in July 2020 has returned over 500% for those readers who took action.

In our earlier book Bear Market Investing Strategies, our broad advice regarding Bitcoin was to add 5-10% in your portfolio as a hedge against a broad global collapse while benefiting from the price increases in the meantime. We suggested this when Bitcoin was around $9,300, and that advice remains unchanged.

What has changed in just the past 12 months is a huge rise in the number of legitimate cryptocurrency projects with solid long-term potential and a working business model (as well as a whole host of memes and scams, but we'll get to those later)

### The Changing Perceptions

What was once strictly the domain of cyberpunks and fiscal anarchists has now been well and truly legitimized. You will find many billionaires and financial institutions are now putting money in crypto. Let's look at these statistics from the past 12 months alone:

- In 2021, venture capitalists deployed a record $19 billion into global crypto startups, which is 3.5 times the previous record set in 2018 (Clark, 2021). Andreesen Horowitz alone announced a brand new $2.2 billion crypto fund in July 2021.
- Cryptos are even making their mark in the ETF market. The first-ever Bitcoin ETF reached $1 billion in assets under management within two days of its launch. It reached this milestone faster than any other ETF in history. (Greifeld, 2021).
- Hollywood movie star Matt Damon is advertising for crypto.com. (Bhasin, 2021)
- Vitalik Buterin was the first of the Crypto Generation to make it to Time's 100 Most Influential People of 2021.
- Sam Bankman-Fried, founder of cryptocurrency derivatives exchange FTX became the world's richest person under 30 (only Mark Zuckerberg was worth more at a younger age).
- Fintech company Stripe, which is the largest private company in Silicon Valley valued at $95 billion, just added the co-founder of crypto firm Paradigm to its board to help build out its crypto team (Clark, 2021).
- New York's newly elected mayor Eric Adams tweeted that he would spend his first three paychecks to invest in Bitcoin as a competition with Miami's mayor Francis Suarez, who tweeted that he's going to take his next salary payment in the cryptocurrency.

**Freeman Publications Crypto History**

The world is finally in a place to take cryptocurrencies seriously. We have been involved with crypto since 2013, and we have seen pretty much everything that Bitcoin and the cryptocurrency market can throw at us. There were dark days when Bitcoin was primarily used to purchase illegal drugs on the dark web.

We remember the hysteria when Bitcoin first rose to $1,000 only to fall 90% in the subsequent months. Then there was the Mt. Gox incident when the website handling 70% of all Bitcoin transactions worldwide was hacked and around 850,000 Bitcoin was stolen.

In 2017 we saw a bull run when cryptocurrency made the mainstream news and Coinbase became the #1 downloaded app in the app store. Obscure coins were gaining 1,000% in a matter of days. Subsequently, in 2018, there was a crash when the entire market lost approximately 80% of its value in just 10 months. All these lead us to today. When we talk about investing in crypto, we know what we are doing because we have seen the highest highs and the lowest lows of the market. We are not approaching it from a point of irrational exuberance or blind optimism.

**It's Not Too Late**

You might be thinking that you have missed out on the best run of crypto. But let me tell you, we are only in the third inning of cryptocurrency right now. Which means there is still a long ways to go yet. There's a great quote from Crypto pioneer, Chris Campbell, which I love that goes "However bullish you are on crypto, you're wrong. You're not bullish enough".

The only adjustment I'd make to that quote is "However bullish you are on crypto... in the long run, you're wrong. You're not bullish enough".

People often accuse me of being a "permabull" – and to them I say, they're right. That doesn't mean I throw money at every company that exists, far from it. Instead, my philosophy revolves around being able to ignore the day-to-day minutia of any financial market (be it stocks, options or crypto) and instead focus on the long game.

I have zero doubt that in 10 years time, cryptocurrency as an asset class will be at least 10x bigger than it is today. I also have zero doubt that we'll experience a 50% pullback in the next 3 years (hell, we may even get one in the next 3 *months*). But during that pullback, I'll just be accumulating more and playing the long game. Because that's how you win. As for which coins I'll be buying, I'll discuss that more in later chapters.

Unfortunately, the mainstream media makes it difficult for you to understand crypto because they are simply focused on showcasing the blatant extremes of this market. I'm talking about the cryptocurrencies created as jokes about dogs, cats, or Elon Musk that can sometimes skyrocket to being worth billions of dollars. We're more focused on the impact it will have an asset class. Both on societal level, and when it comes to your individual wealth.

Here is the straight truth, more individuals will become millionaires due to cryptocurrency than any other asset class in the next decade. A lot of people still think investing in crypto is all about getting lucky or investing in the next joke coin, but hopefully after reading this book, you will see the true potential of cryptocurrency as an asset class.

**The golden rule of crypto:** Never invest more than you can afford to lose. But for reasons we'll lay out in this book, it's also risky to have zero exposure to Bitcoin or any other cryptocurrencies. Relatively speaking, compared with all fiat currencies, Bitcoin is digital beachfront property which is only going to appreciate over time. What most don't understand is the broader crypto market is designed to reward those with conviction, vision and patience. And remember, it's never too late to start thinking in the right direction, which is why we won't be wasting another second.

So if you fear you've missed the crypto boom, don't worry - this trend is just getting started. But you must first do your due diligence in understanding this space inside out. That's how me and my team can help.

Oliver El-Gorr

CEO and Founder, Freeman Publications

London, January 2022

# 1

# WHAT IS CRYPTO AND HOW DOES IT WORK?

Investing in any asset class is a type of commitment, which is why you must know everything about it before you put your hard-earned money in it. For cryptocurrencies, it is even more true because most people are clueless about what they are and how they work. That is why we find it useful to start with the basics. Even if you have some idea about the market, let's brush up on our knowledge quickly before you start worrying about the more complicated aspects of cryptocurrencies.

## What Is Cryptocurrency?

Cryptocurrency is a type of virtual currency which is secured by cryptography so that there is no possibility of counterfeit. While cryptocurrencies have no physical existence, they can still be used as a medium of exchange for goods and services as well. Many companies issue currencies called tokens, which can be traded for the good or service the company deals in.

### A Brief History of Cryptocurrency

While you make think that cryptocurrency started with Bitcoin, that's not exactly true.

Techies have been trying to develop a peer-to-peer electronic currency for decades, but none ever found mainstream adoption day before Bitcoin was created. The original purpose behind the creation of cryptos was to create a decentralized currency that could be used without a central governing institution like a central bank or government. Many financial institutions that act as middlemen in all transactions charge high fees and reap profits in the process. Crypto aimed at removing those encumbrances in the financial system by working around them.

In the 1990s, numerous startups tried to develop a form of digital currency. American cryptographer David Chaum experimented with "blinded cash," which was a form of electronic cash, and used the concept to found his company DigiCash. It was very similar to the modern-day digital currency, having tokens that ensured safe and private transfer of currency between individuals. However, DigiCash failed to achieve any widespread adoption and ultimately the company went bankrupt in 1998.

PayPal then came along and provided a temporary solution to web-based money transfer by attaching itself to the eBay community. It remains one of the biggest payment service providers today, but it could not further the developments of digital currency beyond sending fiat money to an email address.

Then came 2008, when an anonymous entity called Satoshi Nakamoto (whose identity has never been confirmed to this day) first created Bitcoin. The world has not looked back after that. Bitcoin was the only crypto for quite some time until in 2011, crypto enthusiasts started noticing flaws in it. That was when they started developing alternative coins, or altcoins, which aimed at improving the structural and functional design of Bitcoin.

According to CoinMarketCap.com (2021), there are around 15,000 publicly traded cryptocurrencies. Bitcoin still has the highest market cap, followed by Ethereum, Binance Coin, Tether, and Solana.

Cryptocurrencies have low barriers to entry. This means if you have enough time, resources, and a team of skilled people, you can develop your cryptocurrency easily. That is why you can expect to see a significant increase in the number of cryptocurrencies in the future.

**Understanding Blockchain**

Blockchain is the underlying technology that cryptocurrencies use. It is what makes cryptocurrency different from any other currency and the entire traditional financial system, for that matter.

Blockchain is a distributed database that is shared among the nodes of a computer network. It has played a significant role in the development of multiple cryptocurrencies, including Bitcoin. The structure of data stored in a blockchain is quite different from that of a traditional database.

Blockchain helps in maintaining records of all transactions made through cryptocurrency. For example, consider this chain of events.

- You purchase Bitcoin from an exchange.
- Then you use Bitcoin to purchase a luxury watch on the Internet.
- You sell a part of your Bitcoin holdings in exchange for Ethereum.

All these transactions will be recorded in an electronic ledger. The growing list of records, also known as blocks, is linked together using cryptography in such a way that it is very difficult to hack or alter them.

The most important underpinning of blockchain technology is that the data cannot be changed once entered, which makes it easier for individuals to deal with each other directly without the presence of any third party, like a bank or the government.

Each block has a specific storage capacity, and once it is full, it is closed and linked to the long list of blocks that are storing other data. This whole link forms a chain, and that's how this technology gets the name "blockchain." Any information received after that is stored in a new fresh block and hence the chain continues. This technology has been instrumental in maintaining the integrity of cryptocurrencies.

### DECENTRALIZATION—MOST *Important Element of Blockchain*

Decentralization is the reason why blockchain has become such a key part of our economic future.

For example, imagine a company owns a database that is shared across 1000 computers. All those computers are kept inside a single datacenter and everything is controlled from a single point. This sounds fine in theory, but what if there is a power failure or somebody at the company erases some of the data by mistake? Whenever there is one point responsible for managing an entire system, mishaps are bound to happen. Not to mention that the company itself is in complete control of the data. This is the concept of centralization.

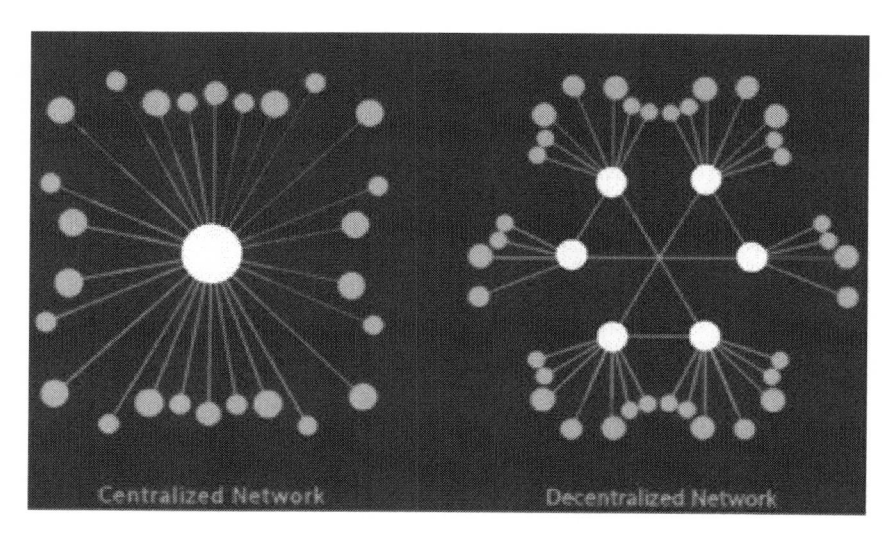

**Figure 1:** The visual difference between a centralized network where all nodes are connected to a single authority, and a decentralized one where no single authority controls the nodes

Blockchain eliminates this problem because it distributes the data across several nodes in various locations. This creates a degree of data redundancy but maintains the fidelity of the data stored within the database. If anyone tries to alter any data or tamper with it, the blockchain system will cross-reference the nodes and simply indicate the one with the incorrect information. This creates transparency and improves the trustworthiness of the system. Most importantly, there is no single point of failure in the system which allows it to have many uses beyond just digital currency, such as legal contracts, auditing software, or inventory management, which we will explain later on in this book.

### WHAT BLOCKCHAIN *Technology Is Not*

If you go through certain books on the blockchain, you will find many authors have compared it with a gigantic, publicly shared Excel worksheet since this is an example that many readers instantly understand. However, this claim is not correct and often leads people to misunderstand the concept entirely. If you have come across this comparison, then let's analyze why it is incorrect.

A shared Excel spreadsheet is a single file and therefore a single and central source of truth. If corrupted or deleted, the shared spreadsheet becomes a single point of failure. As we already discussed, the biggest principle of blockchain is decentralization, which makes it the exact opposite of a shared Excel spreadsheet. The fact that distinguished authors made this comparison shows how little they know about how blockchain works.

### How Blockchain Sets *Cryptocurrency Apart*

The decentralized nature of blockchain technology ensures that the transaction history of any cryptocurrency is accurate and irreversible.

Each node has access to every other node in the decentralized system of the blockchain. Whenever a new block is added, every node on the network is updated with the information of the fresh block. Since all the nodes are interconnected, you can expect complete transparency within the system. This also means there cannot be any forgery within the system, which also prevents a forgery problem that exists with fiat currency (did you know there is approximately $200 Billion in forged fiat currency circulating worldwide right now?).

Even if a cryptocurrency exchange were to be hacked, the blockchain can easily point out which bitcoins were stolen.

Understanding the basics of blockchain is essential to understanding the principle behind cryptocurrency. Beyond just cryptocurrencies, experts from multiple fields predict that blockchain has the capacity to cause great advancements to the entire economy. That is why, before we move further in the discussion about how cryptos work, let's understand a few terms related to blockchain.


### Important Terms

The undifferentiated and sloppy use of the terms "distributed," "decentralized," and "shared" confirms the impression that numerous authors have a serious deficit in understanding the basic concepts about blockchain. It is like a vast ocean, and you can only scratch the surface with such limited knowledge, which is why we have listed the following important terms related to blockchain.

### Encryption

While Dan Brown novels may be the first thing that comes to mind when you hear the word "encryption", it means something different in the context of blockchain. In IT, encryption means writing a code in such a way that only someone with access to its password will be able to read and understand it. All data in a blockchain is encrypted for protection. Data is encrypted using cryptography, which is a set of advanced mathematical principles used to store and transmit data and ensure it is understood by only the sender and recipient of the data.

**Digital Signature**

The entire blockchain network is based on digital signatures because they are used to verify the authenticity of transactions. Whenever you submit data about a transaction, you must do so with the help of your unique digital signature so that every node on the network understands that you are authorized to make the transaction.

| ▽ **HELLOSIGN** | Audit Trail |
| --- | --- |

| | |
| --- | --- |
| TITLE | Employment Contract from Freeman Publications |
| FILE NAME | .pdf |
| DOCUMENT ID | 550ec5dae0d329b9fa36a4ff8da0207e7e888717 |
| AUDIT TRAIL DATE FORMAT | MM / DD / YYYY |
| STATUS | ⊜ Completed |

**Figure 2:** An example of a digital signature in an employment contract

**Asymmetric Cryptography**

First, let us quickly understand what symmetric cryptography is. In the case of symmetric cryptography, there is only one key that can be used to encrypt and decrypt the data. This key can be a number, character, or practically anything. The sender encrypts the message with a key that is shared with the receiver. When the receiver receives the message, they use the same key to decrypt it. This creates a problem because a shared key is not the safest option when it comes to dealing with sensitive information.

That is why blockchain uses asymmetric cryptography. It uses two sets of keys, one to encrypt the data and the other to decrypt it. The two parts of this key pair are called the public key and private key. A public key can be viewed as a username that is accessible to everyone, whilst a private key is more like a password that is not to be shared.

The public key is the one that contains information about the addresses of cryptocurrencies. It can be viewed by anyone, whereas the private key is the one that gives access to the transactions within each address. This is exclusive and can only be accessed by authorized people. Note: We will discuss later on in this book why it is important to always own your private key when it comes to buying and storing cryptocurrency.

Thus, by using asymmetric cryptography, blockchains ensure that sensitive information related to cryptocurrency transaction history cannot be viewed by anyone who is not supposed to view it.


## Mining and Hash

Unlike fiat currency, cryptocurrency is not created by a government or central bank. Instead, it is created mathematically through a process known as mining. In the case of Bitcoin, Satoshi Nakamoto created a protocol in which new bitcoins could only be "mined" by solving complex mathematical algorithms. The way this is done is by using a lot of computer processing power, and the reward for solving the algorithms is receiving Bitcoin in the form of blocks.

Every transaction needs to be validated on the blockchain so that the blocks can be verified as legitimate. To connect each block with the chain, miners need to find out a "hash," or the digital key of the block. Once they find a hash, a new bitcoin is mined and the miners receive their payment in the same cryptocurrency. Before you get excited about the thought of mining Bitcoin from the comfort of your own home, just know that the electricity cost alone will make this an unprofitable endeavor.

. . .

## Consensus Mechanism

In a centralized database, there is a single authority who is responsible for updating, adding, and modifying the records. However, in the case of a decentralized database like blockchain, data is being constantly added by users across the globe. It is very important to have a basis to regulate these transactions since there is no statutory body controlling the system. The consensus mechanism provides several methodologies used to achieve agreement, trust, and security across a decentralized blockchain network. This process ensures that the majority of the participants agree upon the genuineness and legitimacy of the transactions and reach a consensus on the ledger status. Bitcoin employs a consensus mechanism called "Proof-of-Work" (PoW), which requires every node to prove that the work submitted by them is eligible to add new blocks to the blockchain. It is a popular consensus mechanism and is used by many other cryptocurrencies, including Ethereum and Litecoin.

Another popular consensus mechanism is "Proof-of-Stake" (PoS), which gives the responsibility of maintaining the public ledger to a node in proportion to the number of virtual currency tokens held by it. Popular altcoins like Solana, Polkadot, and Cardano use the PoS mechanism. Ethereum also plans to move to a Proof-of-Stake consensus in 2022.

## So What Makes Cryptocurrency Legitimate?

In our first book on the subject *The Only Bitcoin Investing Book You'll Ever Need*, we described the 5 criteria that a currency needs to satisfy in order to achieve legitimacy. Those being

1. Scarcity
2. Divisibility
3. Portability
4. Durability
5. Recognizability

We will now offer a condensed version of that argument

### SCARCITY

One of the most important qualities of any form of money is scarcity. This refers to the ease with which it can be reproduced and originated. The scarcity of an object used as money is important because this ensures supply remains under control and the monetary value of individual units isn't diluted. For example, if everyone had the ability to mint money at home, the value of a dollar bill would decrease.

If everyone was walking around with $100 in their pockets, the prices of everyday goods would readjust to reflect the new monetary reality. Cash buying power would decrease and money itself would be worthless. Fiat money has artificial supply barriers installed thanks to governments guarding their mints zealously.

It also means Bitcoin has a valid case of being treated as money because of its deflationary nature. This is because Bitcoin has a capped supply of 21 million built right into its codebase. Therefore, no more than 21 million Bitcoin can ever be mined, and as of April 2022, around 19.01 million have already been mined (Blockchain.com, 2022) with the last coin projected to be mined around the year 2140.

Because of the limited supply, in theory each Bitcoin becomes more valuable over time, instead of less valuable.

The mining reward algorithm also ensures Bitcoin is hard to replicate. The cost of processing power will steadily increase until there is no value anymore in mining Bitcoin. Even if speculative bubbles pushed the price of Bitcoin to astronomical levels, the hard limit on the number of coins means scarcity is always present.

### DIVISIBILITY

For money to be widely adopted, it needs to be divisible. Divisibility refers to the ease with which a single unit of money can be broken down into smaller units. For example, a dollar bill is extremely divisible. It can be broken down into 100 pennies, four quarters, ten dimes, or any combination of these smaller units.

Divisibility is a key aspect to widespread adoption and is what helped human societies move beyond the barter system. For example, if someone wished to exchange 10 sacks of wheat for five goats, and if both parties had these goods in those quantities, a transaction was possible. However, if someone had just one goat and if the wheat seller insisted on receiving five goats at a minimum, there was no way of seeing the transaction through.

It also explains why other forms of value storage such as gold and silver were eventually abandoned. Gold is extremely valuable but it can be broken down only so much. Silver suffers from the same problem.

Paper money was adopted because it was easy to create divisibility. All it takes to make paper money divisible is to print another number on the bill.

If the price of a gallon of milk rises to $200, that amount can still be broken down into smaller chunks easily. Whether anyone would have money to afford milk at those prices is a different matter. Paper money is always easily divisible.

Bitcoin on the other hand, suffered from a perceived lack of divisibility. In the early days, when a single Bitcoin was worth less than

$100, this wasn't much of an issue. As the value of a single coin rose, and as it became tougher to mine a single coin, there was a clear need to enforce divisibility on the currency.

To clear up a misconception, Bitcoin *is* divisible. In fact, every Bitcoin is divisible to an eighth decimal value. This means one Bitcoin can be broken down into units of 0.00000001 Bitcoin. This unit is also called a Satoshi. Another way of writing this is to say that a single Bitcoin is worth 100,000,000 Satoshis.

Divisibility also ensures that Bitcoin miners can be rewarded in increments, as opposed to spending a lot of effort and receiving nothing in exchange unless they spend resources to mine a single coin. For the user, it means you can purchase fractions of a Bitcoin on an exchange. At the time of writing, $100 would purchase 0.000024BTC.

### Portability

Another key aspect of money is portability. Portability refers to the ease with which it can be carried around for use. Going back to the example of fiat money, it's extremely easy to carry and use. Pieces of paper, which add virtually no encumbrance to the things you normally carry. Still, it's true that a bulging wallet isn't the most comfortable thing to carry, which is why the rise in digital banking and transactions has revolutionized the way we use fiat money.

Contrast this to an alternative store of value such as gold. It's not easy to carry gold bars or bricks around since they're heavy and will almost certainly attract attention.

Bitcoin is even more portable than fiat money is. All it takes to transact in Bitcoin is scanning a QR code that reflects your wallet's address. You can send and receive Bitcoin with a simple scan and this makes it extremely portable. Even if you have an electronic wallet, all it takes is an internet connection and a click of a button to transact in Bitcoin.

· · ·

## DURABILITY

Durability is a tough bar for all forms of money to pass. In fact, most historical forms of money don't pass this test. Including paper money. Durability refers to how easy or tough it is to destroy a form of currency. Paper money is not durable. A dollar bill is easy to carry, but if it's torn or burned, it has no value.

To combat this issue, digital money was introduced through credit and debit cards. These cards are certainly more durable, but they can be stolen, and fraudulent transactions can be carried out easily. Bitcoin's durability is one of the reasons it has reached its currently level of popularity.

It's tough to steal Bitcoin. The only instances of BTC theft have occurred when attackers have gained access to a user's private key.

As for the coins themselves, it's impossible to steal Bitcoin or replicate them elsewhere. For example, no one can remove Bitcoin from your wallet without your consent. The coins cannot be replicated in any way elsewhere. A single Bitcoin is permanent.

What does this mean if a Bitcoin holder loses their private key or forgets it? Simply that they can never gain access to their coins again. Coins that the user has been locked out of cannot be accessed by anyone else or used for any purpose. The nature of the blockchain ensures those coins will remain in place.

Thus, the durability of Bitcoin is extraordinary. It also means users of Bitcoin need to adjust to a new model of thinking about money. They need to guard their keys more closely than the money itself. This isn't the case with paper money, where we don't care much about our wallets as much as we do about their contents. However, as far as economic principles go, Bitcoin is about as durable as any currency can get.

## RECOGNIZABILITY

The recognizability of a form of money is the most important factor in its widespread adoption. For example, everyone on the planet recognizes what a dollar bill looks like and intuitively knows the exchange rate to other forms of money. There are two keys to monetary recognition. The first is that it should be identifiable and the second is that it should be verifiable.

Bitcoin is readily identified thanks to possessing a unique address on the blockchain. All of your coins reside in a wallet that has a specific address. This makes them easily identifiable.

The main difference in recognizability between fiat currency and Bitcoin is how widely accepted it is as a form of money. While Bitcoin is increasing in adoption every single year, it still is nowhere near the level of fiat currency. For this reason alone, we can still consider this an early stage in Bitcoin's adoption journey.

Figure 3 below compares different forms of money across all the factors we've just discussed.

| Traits of Money | Gold | Fiat Currency | Bitcoin |
|---|---|---|---|
| Scarcity | Medium | Low | High |
| Divisibility | Low | Medium | High |
| Portability | Medium | High | High |
| Durability | High | Medium | High |
| Recognizability | Medium | High | Medium |

**Figure 3:** Comparing different forms of currency against the 5 key currency factors

In terms of daily usage, using cryptocurrency is a lot like using a credit card or PayPal, but the exchange takes place through a digital currency instead of the US dollar. You need to use a cryptocurrency wallet, which will enable you to transfer the currency from one account to another. The transaction will only be complete when you provide your private key. So you can conclude that cryptocurrency transactions are safe as long as you don't disclose your private key to anyone else.

Once your transaction is complete, blockchain ensures that the totals will be visible on a public ledger without revealing your identity. Blockchain maintains an electronic ledger of all such transactions, and the data structure inside it ensures immutability. This means that the information inside cannot be altered without altering every block in the chain. This mass change will create a mismatch in the embedded digital signatures. Every new block generated must be verified by all the other nodes in the network, which makes it practically impossible to forge transaction data. This also ensures that there is no "double-spending", which means using the same cryptocurrency which has already been used for a specific transaction. The technical term for this is the 51% protocol or a 51% attack.

A 51% attack involves malicious actors controlling at least 51% of the blockchain, an activity which is extremely costly and time draining, making it a purely hypothetical scenario at this point.

Up until now, we've primarily discussed cryptocurrency and Bitcoin interchangeably. Going forward, we'll be showing you the other uses for cryptocurrency, along with some of the other exciting cryptocurrency projects which are gaining momentum as we enter 2022.

## 2

# WHY THE MAINSTREAM VIEW OF CRYPTO IS OUTDATED

With any cultural phenomenon, the phenomenon itself moves at a faster pace than the commentary surrounding it. In the case of cryptocurrency, we're only now seeing mainstream media sources recognizing the nuances of the crypto market, instead of tainting it with the cyberpunk/financial anarchist edge that it has been tarnished with since Bitcoin's initial rise in 2010.

## The 2 Schools of Thought on How Cryptocurrency Will Exist Going Forward

Crypto enthusiasts or should we say "crypto purists" want to believe that cryptocurrencies are going to revolutionize the entire financial system. This libertarian slant focuses on the decentralized nature of blockchain technology and the desire to exist independent from any government. Whilst there is nothing inherently wrong or harmful with this viewpoint, it is unlikely that this will ever become the reality. Let's examine the 2 schools of thought on the topic.

. . .

### THEORY 1: *Crypto Replaces Fiat Money*

The biggest reason why cryptocurrencies gained popularity in the early 2010s is that there was no central authority controlling them, meaning that digital payments could take place directly between two individuals. Regulatory authorities became wary about their widespread use in the financial system because they lack security and stability.

As we discussed in the previous chapter, there is no doubt about the fact that anything can be used as money if all people agree to it and it fulfills the purpose of serving as a medium of exchange for goods and services.

The decentralized mechanism of cryptocurrencies does not involve any third party between the individuals making the transactions. Crypto enthusiasts like to boast about the fact that since there is no regulatory authority controlling cryptocurrencies, it stays free from corruption. However, somebody who does not have any idea about how the system works will be scared to get involved in such a transaction. You have to remember, the majority of people around the world still have no idea about what cryptocurrencies are and how they work. As of January 2022, less than 3% of the world's population own cryptocurrency. In addition to this, for many, the absence of a bank or government intervention is not a matter of freedom for them. Most people feel safe when there is a regulatory body involved.

Cryptocurrencies are backed by the people who trust in them, whereas the US dollar is backed by the federal government. Even in times of dire crisis, many investors will put their trust in dollars, because their value cannot be denied. New cryptocurrencies called stablecoins are slowly coming into the picture. Even if stablecoins replace traditional currency as a mode of making payments, the supremacy of the US dollar as a store of value is not going to change anytime soon.

Instead, we believe a more likely scenario is the following.

.  .  .

### THEORY 2: *Cryptocurrency Exists in Parallel to Our Current Financial System*

Over the next decade we will see cryptocurrencies peacefully coexisting with the traditional financial system. While Fiat money solves the problem of the barter system, the removal of commodity backing (like the gold standard) from fiat money has greatly increased its inflationary tendencies.

According to data published by the International Monetary Fund, countries like Venezuela face extremely high levels of inflation amounting to almost 1,000,000%.

For context, at an inflation rate of 3.27% (The US average over the past 100 years), it takes a currency around 72 years to lose 90% of its purchasing power. At Venezuela's yearly average, it takes less than 5 months.

This shows how fiat money can collapse even if it is backed by the government. Such widespread collapse leads to the depreciation of cash, which can be addressed with the help of cryptocurrencies and blockchain.

As a technology, blockchain has the potential to have huge positive impacts on all spheres of the economy. There have been developments of a blockchain-based peer-to-peer banking system that will allow the transfer of funds without using fiat money. This is supposed to ease lending and borrowing of blockchain-based assets by anyone who owns a cryptocurrency wallet.

As time passes, cryptocurrency will slowly become a part of our regular financial system and the traces of the same are visible right now. Many custodial exchanges are offering interest payments on widely traded cryptocurrencies like Bitcoin, Ether, and USDC.

Up until now we've only discussed a single use case for cryptocurrency, that being a medium of exchange or a store of value. This is what has driven the rise of Bitcoin since 2010. But the real exciting developments are far beyond this and that's what we'll discuss in the next chapter.

# 3

# UNDERSTANDING THE CRYPTOCURRENCY ECOSYSTEM AS WE ENTER "THE THIRD WAVE" IN 2022

## Phase 1—"Internet Money" and the Rise of Bitcoin

Right from the 1980s and 1990s, there have been efforts to develop a digital currency. We already talked about the failed efforts of DigiCash. After the economic crisis that hit America in 2008, people were exposed to the problems of the traditional financial system. They had lost all trust and were looking for an alternative solution for their financial problems. This troubled economic scenario paved the path for Satoshi Nakamoto to publish a paper called "Bitcoin: A Peer-to-Peer Electronic Cash System," and this can be regarded as the event which truly marked the beginning of the phase I of the cryptocurrency era. From this time onward, a small but loyal group of Bitcoin supporters who traded and mined bitcoins started growing.

### INITIAL TRANSACTIONS

The first-ever Bitcoin transaction took place on January 12, 2009, when Satoshi Nakamoto sent 10 bitcoins to computer programmer Hal Finney. The first US dollar/Bitcoin transaction occurred in 2010 when a developer named Laszlo Hanceyz exchanged 10,000 Bitcoin for US dollars (at a market price of roughly $40) so he could order pizza for his family.

**laszlo**
Full Member

Activity: 199
Merit: 488

**Re: Pizza for bitcoins?**
May 22, 2010, 07:17:26 PM
*Merited by vizique (10), vapourminer (1), Searing (1), BitcoinFX (1), 600watt (1),*

I just want to report that I successfully traded 10,000 bitcoins for pizza.

Pictures: http://heliacal.net/~solar/bitcoin/pizza/

Thanks jercos!

BC: 157fRrqAKrDyGHr1Bx3yDxeMv8Rh45aUet

**Figure 4:** Laszlo Hanceyz's original pizza post on the cryptocurrency forum Bitcointalk

By 2011, Bitcoin hit $1 for the first time, and within 3 months was trading at a price of $29.60.

As Bitcoin's popularity grew, other alternative coins began to see an opportunity to cash in. Rivals like Litecoin, Namecoin, and Swift-coin started entering the scene because they wanted to project themselves as a legitimate currency, unlike Bitcoin, whose primary functions were still limited to transactions on dark websites like Silk Road.

## THE FIRST HALVENING

The first halvening took place in 2012. This was when the rewards for mining a new bitcoin were halved. This event took place again in 2016 and 2020, with the next event halving event projected to take place in early 2024.

Mining a bitcoin was supposed to be a rare event and happened once after every 210,000 blocks. Despite being such a rare phenomenon, miners were stretching themselves and continuously mining more Bitcoin to gain rewards.

That was why the rewards needed to be cut in half to ensure that there were enough Bitcoins available. This was a direct indication of the traction that Bitcoin was getting.

### CRYPTOCURRENCY MAKES *Its Way Into Our Lives*

The world was gradually getting used to cryptocurrencies after they made the headlines. *Time* magazine published an article about them in 2011, which stated that Bitcoin had the potential to challenge traditional currency.

Bitcoin also made its way to popular culture when the US drama series *The Good Wife* titled an episode "Bitcoin for Dummies" in early 2012. Bitcoin's position in our lives was further strengthened with the foundation of Coinbase in June 2012 and the creation of the first Bitcoin ATM in Canada in October 2013.

### THE MT. GOX *Incident*

In 2014, the largest cryptocurrency exchange, Mt. Gox, suddenly filed for bankruptcy after being subject to a huge hacking incident for a while. This was an event of tremendous shock and misery for the owners of 850,000 bitcoins who lost their cryptocurrency during the event. We should note that while exchange hackings can still happen, there is a very simple way to protect your cryptocurrency for ever being subject to this.

Despite these mishaps, the growing popularity of cryptocurrencies, especially Bitcoin, could not be denied.

### Phase 2—The Rise of Ethereum and Legitimacy of Cryptocurrencies as Platforms

Whenever a technology becomes popular, there will be a group of people who will try to find faults within it. In the case of Bitcoin, this fault-finding activity became highly constructive and led to further development in the cryptocurrency space. An unassuming Russian entrepreneur named Vitalik Buterin (often known simply by his first name) may go down as one of the greatest minds in technology history with impacts no smaller than the likes of Steve Jobs or Elon Musk. He saw the biggest limitation of Bitcoin—that it was simply best as a store of value without possessing much utility beyond that.

He was aware of blockchain technology and the enormous potential it had in becoming something much more. This is how Vitalik created Ethereum in 2016, which took the cryptocurrency space in a radical new direction. Ethereum uses blockchain technology, to allow millions of programmers across the world to begin building apps on top of it, allowing them to issue their cryptocurrency assets.

In one of his interviews with Business Insider, Vitalik stated that he felt Bitcoin lacked functionality. He drew up a comparison between a plot key calculator and a smartphone, saying that Bitcoin was the former and he aspired to create the latter. A plot key calculator did only one thing perfectly, but since people had all kinds of dynamic needs, they wanted to do all sorts of things on a given platform.

This second phase in 2016 allowed cryptocurrencies to become more than what even the greatest visionaries could have imagined mere years before.

## How Does Ethereum Work?

Since the central technology is blockchain, the working of Ethereum is similar to that of Bitcoin. It has a distributed public ledger and every participant in the Ethereum network has an identical copy of the network, which constantly gets updated as new blocks are added to the chain. There is no central regulatory authority, and the entire ledger is maintained through a decentralized system. When a new cryptocurrency is mined in this network after confirming the validity of the transactions, the miner gets rewarded with a cryptocurrency token called Ether. The uses of Ether are similar to Bitcoin in the sense that they can be used to buy legitimate goods and services. However, what makes Ethereum unique is that users can build applications to run on the blockchain like software runs on a computer. These applications can store and transfer personal data and even handle complex financial transactions.

### DIFFERENCE BETWEEN ETHER and Ethereum

Ether is a cryptocurrency that can be used for transactions or as an investment whereas Ethereum is the blockchain network on which Ether operates. However, the Ethereum network has a variety of other functions in addition to just issuing Ether. On the Ethereum network, you will be able to host your decentralized applications. For example, if your company deals with a lot of sensitive data that you don't want to host on servers owned by Amazon or Google, you can instead use the Ethereum blockchain, which will give you complete control over your data without having to report it to another third party. Ethereum was the first in this space to provide such unique features to companies.

### SMART CONTRACTS

The biggest game-changer that set Ethereum apart in the entire cryptocurrency space is the creation of self-executing contracts, better known as smart contracts. These are tools that automatically execute contracts provided that certain conditions are met, and the compensation is paid in Ether.

As you can imagine, smart contracts use blockchain technology and Ethereum was one of the pioneers in this space. In the case of a regular contract, if one party violated the terms and conditions, the other could take them to court and settle the matter. Smart contracts eliminate the possibility of violation because the blockchain code is structured in such a way that the conditions will automatically be enforced. Here are some of the popular applications of smart contracts:

- Multisignature accounts, which allow funds to be

transferred only when the designated percentage of people agree to it.

- Encoding financial agreements, which enables management between users. For example, if there is an insurance contract between two parties, the rules regarding redemption and surrender of insurance can be encoded into a smart contract.
- Working as a software library and allowing smart contracts to work in a chain rather than in isolation.
- Use financial, social, or political data and create agreements based on them. Smart contracts work very well in the execution of derivatives contracts and encode all rules of derivatives into their program.
- Storing important information. When you are using Ethereum blockchain to store data like membership records or domain information, it stays immutable and can't be erased.

Although it is still in its initial phase, Ethereum smart contracts opened doors to many new possibilities, and they have the potential to completely change the technological scenario.

```
 1 contract Puzzle{
 2   address public owner;
 3   bool public locked;
 4   uint public reward;
 5   bytes32 public diff;
 6   bytes public solution;
 7
 8   function Puzzle() //constructor{
 9     owner = msg.sender;
10     reward = msg.value;
11     locked = false;
12     diff = bytes32(11111); //pre-defined difficulty
13   }
14
15   function(){ //main code, runs at every invocation
16     if (msg.sender == owner){ //update reward
17       if (locked)
18         throw;
19       owner.send(reward);
20       reward = msg.value;
21     }
22     else
23       if (msg.data.length > 0){ //submit a solution
24         if (locked) throw;
25         if (sha256(msg.data) < diff){
26           msg.sender.send(reward); //send reward
27           solution = msg.data;
28           locked = true;
29         }}}}
```

**Figure 5:** A simple smart contract which rewards users for solving a puzzle (Source: Adrian Colyer)

### *Ethereum Vs. Bitcoin: Which Is More Important?*

Since Ethereum was created to overcome the potential limitations of Bitcoin, it can be said that as a technology, Ethereum has much more to offer. While Bitcoin remains the most valuable cryptocurrency at a current market cap of around $800 billion at the time of writing, it is followed by Ethereum which has a market cap of just under $400 billion. Given its widespread applications, Ethereum is capable of creating a huge disruption in the cryptocurrency space.

Smart contracts are a foundational stepping stone to decentralized autonomous organizations (DAOs). If you look at an organization, it can be considered as a complex web of contracts that performs functions like buying and selling things, hiring labor, negotiating deals, creating and balancing budgets, and generating profits. The size and scope might vary, but the main structure is the same for all entities. If these functions can be coded into a smart contract, we can have pieces of software hiring new people within years.

Ethereum's rise in early 2016 sparked the next wave of the cryptocurrency revolution which gave birth to the first batch of higher value altcoins. Coins such as Ripple (XRP), Litecoin (LTC) and Cardano (ADA) all came to prominence during this time and the overall crypto market value increased 100-fold from $7 billion in January 2016 to $800 Billion in January 2021. This was despite a 2-year bear market in 2018 and 2019.

## Phase 3—Crypto Goes Mainstream

In 2017, the value of Bitcoin hit $10,000 for the first time. The world was seeing steady growth for quite some time, but this was an important landmark, and it finally enabled cryptocurrency to enter into the mainstream commercial sector. By now, the early investors had gained bragging rights because the bitcoins they were holding had multiplied in value. New investors were looking for an opportunity to enter the market while blockchain was seeing a boom in the fintech sector.

This was the time when cryptocurrency received its stamp of authentication and big corporations started investing heavily in cryptocurrency. Ethereum was at the center of all these developments due to its additional features that enhanced speed and improved efficiency. Microsoft launched its first blockchain service so users could comply and deploy Ethereum smart contracts. Other Fortune 500 companies like Amazon, IBM, JP Morgan, Walmart, and Chase also entered into Ethereum investments soon after, which marked its entry into some of the most prominent industries.

### Crypto Entering Into Cloud Computing

Cloud computing is the process of storing and sharing resources and data by using a network of remote servers on the Internet rather than your personal computer. It suffered from multiple limitations, many of which were successfully removed after being integrated with blockchain technology. Cloud computing is using cryptocurrencies and blockchain to develop a highly specialized web platform called Web 3. Web 3 is the upcoming third generation of the internet, where websites and apps will be able to process information in a smart human-like way through technologies like machine learning and big data, all in a decentralized manner. This decentralized blockchain technology will connect the data and unlike the current generation of internet platforms, won't rely on centralized management. Once the new platform is up and running, we can expect to witness the blooming of a symbiotic relationship between cryptocurrencies and Web 3.

### Crypto Influences the Banking Sector

The financial sector did not waste much time to realize the massive impact blockchain could have on its efficiency. Data inside a blockchain network is immutable and there is not much scope of making an error, which reduces the chances of committing fraud. These features make blockchain an extremely suitable option for any financial system. Not only that, we saw the advent of an alternative financial ecosystem called decentralized finance where consumers could buy, sell, lend, and borrow cryptocurrencies. This would enable users to make cryptocurrency transactions outside the traditional banking and financial regulations.

Cryptocurrency lending has emerged to become quite popular in the decentralized finance space. Since the lender does not have to undergo a credit score check for obtaining a crypto-backed loan, it is a convenient option for people with poor credit history. These are asset-backed loans where you will be pledging your cryptocurrencies.

These loans are available on platforms like Binance, BlockFi, and Celsius.

### CRYPTO *and the Gaming Sector*

The gaming industry is famous for following all kinds of trends. Whenever a game becomes popular, others try to copy it because certain game formats are conducive to making a lot of money. An example of this would be games like Fortnite and PUBG sparking many clones in the Battle Royale genre.

Investors of game companies now desperately want the creators to use blockchain technology in their games because a decentralized database is very attractive for them. Following this craze, a game called Axie Infinity was created by Vietnamese studio Sky Mavis. It is a trading and battling game that allows players to collect, breed, raise, battle, and trade cattle called "Axies," which are non-fungible tokens or NFTs (more on that later). You need at least three Axies to start, so the game is minting money right from the very beginning.

The modern cryptocurrency scene is changing rapidly as blockchain makes its way into mainstream industries. Recently, the European Blockchain Expo was hosted in Amsterdam, and to my surprise, there was something very different from previous Blockchain conferences. There was a paradigm shift in the nature of the crowd.

Before, blockchain conferences were mostly filled with nerdy college-goers or recent grads in shorts and flip-flops. However, this time I noticed they were replaced by executives from multi-billion-dollar corporations like Shell, Pfizer, Boston Consulting Group, Coca-Cola, Aon, and Mercedes Benz. Cryptocurrency is no longer a passion project of computer geeks. The barrier has broken and the cryptocurrency market has gone mainstream.

# 4

# THE TRUTH ABOUT THE STATE OF
# THE ALTCOIN MARKET IN 2022

While Bitcoin was long considered the only cryptocurrency, the crypto ecosystem has now seen a parabolic rise in the altcoin market.

If you take a look at the database at CoinMarketCap, you will find that there are thousands of cryptocurrencies listed on the platform (16,602 at the time of writing). Many of them have strange names like Lil Doge Floki, BunsCake, and GreenMoonZilla. These sound like characters from a children's book, don't they? This is yet another reason why the mainstream media often portrays cryptocurrency as some sort of joke.

## So What Are Altcoins?

We already discussed a bit about altcoins in Chapter 1, but let's get into further detail. Altcoins get their name from the phrase "alternative to Bitcoin," because that was how they came into existence.

Any cryptocurrency apart from Bitcoin can be called an altcoin. This includes popular coins like Ethereum, Stellar, Polkadot, Monero, Cardano, Solana, Dogecoin, and Shiba Inu. Altcoins were created to overcome the limitations of Bitcoin, and some have been successful in doing so to a certain extent.

Since they are technologically different from Bitcoin, the creators of altcoins are promoting competition and allowing others to further develop more cryptocurrencies. For example, many altcoins facilitate lower transaction fees than Bitcoin, which is why they are becoming more popular among the masses.

On top of this, many ordinary investors see the price of Bitcoin ($48,000 at the time of writing) as being a prohibitive entry point. While this isn't the case (see our divisibility argument from earlier), many creators of altcoins are aware of this situation, and that is why the market is being flooded with multiple altcoins which are seemingly more affordable. Even if these facts make altcoins sound intriguing, their value is highly volatile and the vast majority are subject to scams and frauds. That is why it's crucial to do your due diligence before you start investing in them.

### THE 4 TYPES *of Altcoins*

Altcoins are usually classified based on their functionalities and consensus mechanisms, but one altcoin can fall under more than one category.

### Transaction Coins

Transaction coins function similar to what we saw with Bitcoin in its early days in that these are designed to be used as an exchange of value for goods and services. Most early altcoins that came to prominence fell into this category with Namecoin being the first significant one in 2011. Some examples are Litecoin (LTC), Monero (XMR), and ZCash (ZEC).

**Stablecoins**

Volatility is an integral part of cryptocurrencies, but that's why stablecoins exist. Stablecoins are cryptocurrencies that have their values pegged to a real world asset such as fiat currency or precious metals. These assets act as a buffer and protect the value of the stablecoins from declining excessively. The underlying assets ensure a floor value for the stablecoins. Stablecoins add an additional layer of legitimacy to the crypto market as for mass adoption, we must move away from pure speculation and volatility. Because to use cryptocurrency as a store of value, or as a substitute for traditional money requires a degree of stability. This is why stablecoins, which provide the best of both worlds, have long been considered to be the holy grail of cryptocurrencies.

Lael Brainard, a member of the Federal Reserve Board of Governors said "Stablecoins aspire to achieve the functions of traditional money without relying on confidence in an issuer—such as a central bank—to stand behind the money."

Stablecoins have received significant adoption from the traditional finance community. Financial giant Visa also announced in 2021 that it would begin to settle certain transactions on its network in USDC by using the Ethereum blockchain. Visa is a giant in the payment processing industry, which is why this announcement acted as a huge boost for altcoins.

Examples of important stablecoins are Tether's USDT, Maker-DAO's DAI, and the USD Coin (USDC).

## SECURITY TOKENS

Security tokens are the digital version of the stocks traded on a stock exchange. They offer ownership of a company in the form of equity and even have dividend payouts in regular frequencies. Investors are drawn to these altcoins because they offer a prospect of price appreciation and comparative stability. In 2021, Bitcoin wallet firm Exodus completed a Securities and Exchange Commission-qualified Reg A+ token offering and sold $75 million shares of common stock to be converted to tokens on the Algorand blockchain (Frankenfield, 2021). This marked a historic event since it was the first time a US-based issuing company offered digital asset security as equity.

UTILITY TOKEN

Utility tokens are used to purchase any utilities or services, redeem rewards, or pay network fees over a specific network. You can look at these as the cryptocurrency equivalents of public transport passes or gift cards. They do not pay dividends or provide ownership like security tokens. Examples of utility tokens are Filecoin (FIL), a utility token that is used to purchase storage space on a cloud and Civic (CVC) which is used for identity verification.

## The One Type of Altcoin to Stay Away From

In every booming market, there are always going to be scammers. After all, sunny places attract shady people. It happened in the dot-com boom. Companies with no business model went public just to make the founders and early insiders rich. It also happened in the housing boom, where a lot of scammers got rich. And now, it's happening in the cryptocurrency boom as well.

## Meme Coins

Look, we all love a good laugh, but the crypto space is now rife with people investing their hard earned money into coins that started as jokes. Coins like Dogecoin (DOGE), Shiba Inu (SHIB), and Safe-Moon (SAFEMOON), basically anything with a dog, or reference to getting rich in the name can be considered a meme coin. If you want to own $10 worth of Dogecoin as a fun joke then go ahead, but please don't invest in any of these coins expecting any kind of ROI.

Remember that Bitcoin and Ethereum, were both created to answer real-world issues. The ultimate objective is for them to be widely accepted by merchants, resulting in the creation of a new kind of decentralized currency that will revolutionize a range of sectors.

On the other hand, meme coins currently serve no real-world use, and the majority of them were established for profit. Many developers of these coins sell quickly once the prices rise in order to earn a rapid profit because meme coins have no practical utility.

**Figure 6:** A prime example of what we consider meme coins. (Source: coinmarketcap.com)

As the meme coin market grows, you should be cautious that certain projects may try to take advantage of the enthusiasm to defraud traders. For example, in only one week, Squid Game (SQUID), a meme currency based on the famous Netflix program of the same name, increased by almost 86,000%. However, the development team immediately pulled the rug out from under them, causing the price to collapse by 99%. Worse, holders have been barred from selling their SQUID tokens.

So please, next time you come across a news article highlighting an obscure coin that went up 10,000% in a day - do some simple due diligence before you invest. Rule #1 of crypto investing is the same as Rule #1 of stock investing - don't lose money.

## The Psychology Behind Successful Altcoin Investing

Whenever a certain asset class starts rising, early adopters begin making a lot of money, which is exactly what happened with Bitcoin. Bitcoin was the first cryptocurrency available to the public, and people who understood its significance (and had the risk tolerance to hold onto their investment during downturns), made significant profits.

When the wider market becomes became aware of this, they are often full of regret in having missed out on the biggest boom of Bitcoin.

This was the first trigger that prompts bad actors to do something about this missed opportunity. They tapped into these feelings and filled the market with sub-par coins which had no utility. Most of these coins did not have the fundamentals to provide long term wealth for theirs owners, but for many new investors, they didn't care, they just wanted to make a quick buck.

For them, it was all about entering this buzzing new space by investing as little as possible. Think about a company splitting its stocks. Suppose you are holding one share worth $100 and the company decides to go for a four-to-one stock split. Now you will be holding four shares worth $25 each.

The psychology behind the altcoin craze is quite similar. The rising value of Bitcoin seemingly makes it inaccessible to the masses, which is why they want to go for the "cheaper" alternatives. After all, why own 0.00012 units of one asset when you can own 12,000 units of another? It's a natural human tendency to want to own more of some-thing, even if the total monetary value is the same.

However, the problem is that the vast majority of altcoins are still fraudulent and have little to no fundamental value backing up their price. Recently, a cryptocurrency called DeTrade was making rounds of the market. It had a very good coin development team who made high claims on LinkedIn, and they had glorious articles posted on popular news websites. The CEO had even created and posted a video of how the cryptocurrency would use its unique technology to disrupt the entire market. One of my friends came to know about DeTrade from a Telegram group he was a part of and was convinced about its potential. He invested around $2,000 in it, only to realize later on that the entire thing was a scam. The DeTrade team had created fake LinkedIn profiles and misleading videos to trick people into putting money on it. My friend lost only $2,000, but DeTrade made off with more than $2 million worth of investor money (Van Boom, 2021).

Here is the problem with 95% of altcoins: the majority of them fit into one or more of these 3 "coin killer" categories

1. Have an unlimited supply - meaning that more of them can just be printed whenever, leaving them subject to massive inflation. As a sub-point to this, stay away from pre-mined coins like DASH or XRP
2. Centralized - issued by a single company or institution, going against the core philosophy of cryptocurrenc (XRP also fits this criteria)
3. Don't solve a problem that Bitcoin doesn't already solve. The majority of coins don't solve *any* real world problem. Plus if a coin is trying to solve *too many* problems then that's also a red flag

## Altcoins of the Future

One thing that Bitcoin maximalists have gotten wrong is that there is no single solution in cryptocurrency.

Many solutions may exist, hence why there may be more than one winner as cryptocurrency evolves.

To make a comparison to the fiat currency world, America has dollars. Britain has pounds. In fiat currencies, both currencies have "won." The problem these two currencies are solving is that Americans might trust the U.S. government and Britons might trust the British government.

Until now, geographic boundaries have created new currencies.

But geographic boundaries are man-made and require middlemen. In crypto terms, we aren't worried about geographical boundaries, instead we are more focused on the utility of the tokens themselves. Ethereum might be used for hosting decentralized applications, whereas Filecoin might be used for transactions that have a specific storage application.

Therefore "crypto boundaries" are determined by real problems being solved rather than artificial geographic boundaries.

While the majority of the 16,000+ cryptocurrencies listed online are still complete scams with no utility, we are in a different ecosystem than we were even at the beginning of 2021.

This is why as we enter 2022, there are now multiple cryptocurrency projects which do have decent fundamentals, and we would consider long-term investments in them.

- **Ethereum:** Right now, Ethereum has the largest market cap after Bitcoin, which is why it can be considered as the most valuable altcoin. At the time of writing there are more than 3,000 applications running on the Ethereum network, including prominent ones like MakerDAO, Axie Infinity and Uniswap. The growth of these platforms has led to Ethereum's 15 fold rise in the past 4 years alone. And while the protocol has its own scaling problems, we still believe it has a positive future going forward
- **Polkadot:** Outside of Bitcoin and Ethereum, Polkadot was the most held crypto asset by hedge funds in 2021. The platform works on a sharded multichain network, which means it can process multiple transactions by integrating across different blockchains. This parallel processing system helps in improving the scalability of the system which has made Polkadot the development platform of choice for Web3 developers.
- **Aave:** Aave (pronounced aah-vay) is a decentralized lending and borrowing platform. After raising $25 million from VC firms like Blockchain Capital, it quickly became

the largest DeFi app on the Ethereum protocol in early 2021. Users simply deposit their crypto (like ETH) and earn interest on it from borrowers.

- **Cardano:** The unique multi-layer architecture sets Cardano apart from other cryptocurrencies. It is slowly developing a powerful and flexible blockchain network that is expected to compete with Ethereum very soon. Investors are particularly interested in its low energy levels and fast transaction processing. It has shown modest but stable growth for the last few years and could do big things in 2022.

ALL 4 OF these coins can be purchased on Coinbase and stored on a Ledger hardware Wallet. We have free video tutorials for both of these on our YouTube channel which you can find at

HTTPS://FREEMANPUBLICATIONS.COM/CRYPTOTUTORIALS

AUTHOR'S NOTE: We have received a number of emails from readers who are concerned with both the Ledger and Trezor hardware wallets being Made in China. While we do not see this being a security threat, if you do believe that is the case, then the best alternative is the BitBox02 which is made in Switzerland.

Although there are thousands of altcoins in the market, these are the relatively safer ones because of their current adoption and real world utility. However as a reminder, the cryptocurrency market is unpredictable. Whichever coins you do or don't invest in, expect a lot of volatility. If you've never invested in crypto before, drops of 10% in a single day are relatively common, with drops of 30% in a month a common occurrence as well.

# 5

# TRILLION DOLLAR DISRUPTER - THREE INDUSTRIES BEING DISRUPTED BY CRYPTOCURRENCY

After the recent European Blockchain Expo, it was clear to me that cryptocurrency and blockchain technology is becoming a key part of most industries. Many companies are now looking at Bitcoin or other cryptocurrencies as a viable investment and a means for executing transactions. As blockchain-enabled smart contracts are being used in various applications, cryptocurrencies are slowly penetrating big corporations and their important functions. Eventually cryptocurrency will become an integral part of the business world, but right now we can talk about three industries that are being seriously disrupted by crypto.

## Finance and Banking

Anyone over the age of 30 will remember the massive financial crisis of 2008 and how the banking sector played a role in manufacturing it. Bitcoin was one of the direct responses to that crisis because the people were fed up with a central authority making financial decisions that could adversely affect the fortune of countries. The decentralized system and peer-to-peer technology of Bitcoin had shown the potential of disrupting the entire banking system. The creator of

Bitcoin mentioned it as a "version of electronic cash" that allows "online payments to be sent from one party to another without going through a financial institution." (*What is Bitcoin?*, Satoshi Nakamoto)

If you consider the problems that Bitcoin can solve within a financial system, the following points come to mind:

- Since Bitcoin works through a blockchain, the underlying cryptography ensures that there is no double spending.
- Despite being decentralized, Bitcoin is relatively safer. The consensus mechanism prevalent within every cryptocurrency network makes it very difficult to conduct a fraudulent transaction. If there is a disagreement from one node, the entire transaction can be invalidated.
- The decentralized system eliminates the need for intermediaries.

Bitcoin was exhibiting all these features right from its inception, but the financial sector never looked at it as a threat until its value started skyrocketing. However, the bigger development came with the introduction and gradual evolution of stablecoins.

### What Role Do Stablecoins Play in This Disruption?

We already discussed what stablecoins are in the previous chapter. Stablecoins are a powerful innovation because they fulfill the "currency" mandate of cryptocurrencies by eschewing price volatility in favor of mechanisms that maintain a peg to fiat currencies through various blockchain designs. All circulating stablecoins maintain a reasonable simplistic model at a high level and aim at maintaining parity between assets and outstanding liabilities. Stablecoin growth is exploding, which is evident from their meteoric overall market cap growth from roughly $6 billion at the beginning of 2020 to the current mark of over $100 billion a little less than 2 years later.

· · ·

## TRADITIONAL FINANCE Vs. Stablecoins

Before we start talking about how stablecoins can disrupt the traditional financial system, it is important to understand the function of a central bank in the economy. Central banks use various monetary policies to control the money supply and interest rates. They operate through the open market using various levers like cutting interest rates, curbing bank reserve requirements, and buying up treasuries to achieve their desired mandates. Directed action in the market has collateral effects across the interest rate curve, with the goal usually being the expansion of money supply, stimulated spending, which in theory leads to long term economic growth.

Algorithmic stablecoins employ a similar model but replace the suits and ties in boardrooms with algorithms that digest, calibrate, and dynamically adjust to market forces in real-time. They are cryptocurrencies that track the price of other assets and currencies. Crypto dollars exist to merge the low volatility characteristics of sovereign currencies like the dollar with the decentralized settlement assurance of the public blockchains. In short, they allow you to move and settle arbitrary amounts of fiat currency anywhere over the Internet with strong fidelity and few of the encumbrances of the traditional banking system.

A section of economists hold these stablecoins in high regard because they believe stablecoins can result in a cost-effective, safe, and more competitive payment gateway that works in real time. Stablecoins can also connect the underbanked or unbanked sections of society through their digital reach.

## How ARE Governments Reacting to This Disruption?

Governments all around the world have varied opinions about the rise of stablecoins. Some of them want to project them as nothing but the next big scam, while others are in the process of figuring how to integrate them into the wider economy.

The pros and cons of stablecoins can be debated to great extents, but their growing popularity cannot be ignored anymore. Gary

Gensler, the chair of the U.S. Securities and Exchange Commission, commented at a conference in August 2021 that the time had come to regulate the cryptocurrency markets. The chair of the Federal Reserve, Jerome Powell, urgently called for regulating stablecoins. Treasury Secretary Janet Yellen even stated that stablecoins "had the potential to support beneficial payment options".

People of such high economic significance only comment about things that *really* matter. These comments indicate that the government views stablecoins as a legitimate digital currency which is going to play an important role in the future of global finance.

The Federal Reserve governor has indicated the government's plan to explore a Central Bank Digital Currency as a response to the rising popularity and strength of stablecoins. A CBDC is a type of fiat currency in digital form. Since it is issued by the central bank of a country, it has the faith of the issuing country's government. CBDCs are still undergoing developments in various parts of the world, and once done, they are expected to simplify the implementation of fiscal and monetary policy.

The government's initiative in developing CBDCs proves the fact that they are intimidated by the rapid development of stablecoins. They might look at it as an act of countering the stablecoin, but in reality, they are acknowledging its existence and rising importance.

### THE GROWTH of the Terra Ecosystem and Luna

New stablecoins are coming into existence every other day, and Terra is one which has gained popularity quite quickly. Terra is a blockchain payment platform for algorithmic stablecoins. It helps the users to save, spend, trade, or exchange Terra stablecoins instantly on its blockchain. The main purpose of the Terra protocol is to track the price of any fiat currency such as euros or US dollars. The network has two main cryptocurrency tokens, Terra and Luna. Let's briefly discuss their features:

- **Terra:** This is the token that tracks the prices of individual currencies. Each token tracking a particular currency is named after that currency. For instance, the Terra token that tracks the Special Drawing Rights issued by the IMF is called TerraSDR and the one that tracks dollars is called TerraUSD.

- **Luna:** Luna absorbs the price volatility of Terra, acting as the staking token. It is used for governance and mining. Luna's worth is linked to Terra's usage.

### DeFi 2.0

One huge crypto trend which hasn't made its way to mainstream reporting is DeFi 2.0. This is the second generation of decentralized finance protocols that expanded on the utility of the first generation ones which gave us things like crypto lending, yield farming and market making abilities on the blockchain.

The majority of DeFi 1.0 limitations were based around the limitations of the protocols themselves, which led to a poor user experience (making onboarding difficult for all but the most dedicated of enthusiasts). Much of this revolves around the scaling issues that Ethereum has faced in the past 3 years, as many DeFi 1.0 projects were built on Ethereum.

DeFi 2.0 aims to do for the DeFi movement, what Coinbase did for the mainstream cryptocurrency exchange movement. Provide a more streamlined, simple solution which is more in-line with how consumers are used to interacting with services online.

We see DeFi 2.0 as having far more business to business utility, with projects like OlympusDAO aiming to build a decentralized reserve currency. The real gamechanger here is being able to scale crypto lending operations (because right now the problem is that there are simply more lenders than borrowers) as well as provide a more consistent cash flow for the ecosystem, which in turn will reduce volatility.

DeFi 2.0 will also mean more competition for Ethereum going forward, with Solana (SOL) being a frontrunner due to its low-cost, high speed, and scalable alternative to Ethereum. These inherent features, paired with composability, have helped Solana cement itself as a choice platform of DeFi 2.0.

### OTHER AREAS *of the Financial Sector Where Blockchain Can Make Its Mark*

The gradual rise of altcoins and blockchain technology has made it clear that this will leave a significant mark on the financial sector. The benefits of this technology make it a perfect fit for a variety of financial operations, and that is why we have listed the following sectors which we believe will be positively affected by blockchain and crypto:

- **Stock Market Settlements:** Blockchain is set to revolutionize stock market settlements by reducing the time taken for transaction processing and improving the efficiency of trading. It will result in lower operational costs, and smart contracts will ensure greater efficiency and security. NASDAQ already uses blockchain for private placement, and the London Stock Exchange is exploring areas where they can apply the technology.
- **Asset Management:** With the growth of global trade, the importance of asset management is increasing all over the world. In fact, the asset management industry is among the fastest-growing ones in the world and is expected to grow by $150 trillion by 2025 (Jain, 2020). Right now, the asset management network follows a centralized system that enables the users to view the assets held on a real-time basis. However, the system is migrating to a distributed ledger system for easier access and management. This is where blockchain technology comes into the picture. This system will help in the faster processing of cross-border transactions and ensure error-free processing of data.
- **Efficient Payments:** Blockchain technology can bring

about serious improvements in the payment processing systems of banks or other financial institutions. Transactions that used to take more than a week to be processed can now be instantly transferred with the help of blockchain. Since it removes the requirements of intermediaries and money can be transferred directly between individuals, blockchain will save time and money. Central banks of many countries are trying to implement a distributed ledger system that will improve settlement fidelity and operational risk.

- **Compliance Processes:** Know Your Customer (KYC) is an essential element of the entire financial sector. Every country has elaborate KYC compliance requirements, which create a huge workload for the people employed in these institutions. Using blockchain services like KYC-chain will help the companies to streamline this process. Bankers will be able to check the KYC details on a real-time basis, which would subsequently reduce data duplication and improve work efficiency. The customer identification process will be automated and banks will have a digital source of ID that can be accessed on a decentralized platform by any authorized personnel.
- **Fraud-Free Insurance Claim Management:** Blockchain is helping the insurance industry by developing a fraud-free system where claims can be sorted automatically with the help of smart contracts. It links all concerned parties of an insurance contract, like broker, client, insurer, and insured, resulting in efficient and transparent communication.

## Crypto Cloud Computing

We briefly discussed Web 3 in a previous chapter. In this section, I would like to tell you a bit more about our views about Web 3 and what it means for cryptocurrency investors. It is my prediction that the Web 3 era is the third phase of the crypto market and it can make cryptocurrencies more mainstream than ever.

I believe that it has the potential to be an event that grows the value of the entire cryptocurrency market 100x from here. Mind you, it won't happen overnight, but I think the expected ramifications are massive.

### THE RISE of Web 3

Chris Dixon, a partner at Andreesen Horowitz and considered one of the smartest venture capitalists of this generation, speaks very highly about Web 3 and the future it holds for us. In a 2021 blog post titled *Why Web3 Matters*, Dixon surmised:

*"We are now at the beginning of the web 3 era, which combines the decentralized, community-governed ethos of web 1.0 with the advanced, modern functionality of web2.0".*

Right now, we still largely exist in a web 2.0 world where giant corporations own huge chunks of the internet, and your data, Google and Facebook being the 2 which immediately spring to mind. While these companies have been a net positive for society over the past 2 decades, we are now seeing the tide shifting against them, and a further move towards decentralization.

Web 3 facilitates a decentralized platform using blockchain technology which allows users to use the internet without their data being stored in a centralized hub or owned by a single corporation. The biggest problem with centralized platforms is that they limit innovation after a certain point. These platforms are completely dependent upon third-party complements like developers, creators, and businesses. The centralized networks work in such a way that they need to keep on extracting data from their users and former partners if they wish to grow.

For the third parties involved, this indicates a switch from cooperation to competition, which makes them wary. Chris Dixon says that these issues are making the best entrepreneurs, developers, and investors turn away from centralized platforms. However, this is good news for Web 3, because these shortcomings of Web 1 and Web 2 are paving the way for the digital superiority of Web 3. Web 3 has decentralized ownership and control, and tokens allow users to own a piece of the Internet.

Web 3 marks the beginning of an era when cryptocurrency companies can compete with and replace the largest technology companies in the world through the use of blockchain technology.

Here's what it looks like in practice. A "Phase 3" crypto called Internet Computer (ICP) mimics many of the most advanced features of major cloud services like Amazon's AWS and Microsoft's Azure. So, you can deploy websites, enterprise IT systems, and Internet services much like you would with Amazon or Microsoft's cloud hosting. However, here's what's going to bend your mind a little bit.

With the Internet Computer, you can deploy your code directly to the Internet itself through blockchain, and there will be no intermediary like Amazon or Microsoft. This technology that was pioneered by Bitcoin is hitting a new inflection point in its capabilities by allowing people to lend their computing resources.

If you're still having doubts about why Web 3 is the future, here are a few reasons why they matter:

- The decentralized system makes societies efficient by removing the third parties and reducing the cost associated with managing these intermediaries. This will result in greater value creation for the people who are the real users and developers of data.
- The new mesh of peer-to-peer communication will enable organizations to become more resilient to change.
- Sharing of data between humans, enterprises, and machines will become more efficient through the privacy and security of the blockchain network.
- Tokenized digital assets will enable the users to own their data and digital footprints.

### THETA AND DECENTRALIZED *Video Streaming*

Theta (THETA) blockchain provides a decentralized platform and a "Phase 3" crypto which provides a solution to delivering video content across the Internet without depending on data centers. Most Internet traffic is filled with video content, and the numbers will only continue to rise in the future because everyone is looking for real-time updates about what's going on. Websites providing video-streaming content have mostly used a centralized system, which has been largely dependent upon the data centers located close to you. Over time, this has become a problem due to connectivity issues and pressure on the system has made the quality of streaming slow and choppy. A possible remedy to this might be a content delivery system where a group of servers will be dispersed so that the system is not burdened too much, but this can be a costly affair.

Theta is building a cryptocurrency solution to this problem by setting up a peer-to-peer network that aims at utilizing unused bandwidth. When you are trying to view content on the Theta network, part of the data will come from the network itself and the rest will be delivered from the unused computing power of other nodes. This is not some pie-in-the-sky dream because the co-founders of YouTube and Twitch TV are on the Theta team along with backing from Sony, Google, and Samsung. This makes it a massive market opportunity. The means of earning profit is not through a company like Fastly but a cryptocurrency like Theta.

In my opinion, the bottom line is that we are now starting to see Web 3 projects that are seeing real world utility, and will profitably reward investors. We have the option of waiting until the market matures and bringing it to our readers when there is potentially less risk but also a lot less upside.

The other option is to alert our members about these developments when they're in what we believe is truly the "ground-floor" stage. I hope readers would appreciate us doing so because we are certain this could transform the industry drastically.

## Crypto in Video Games

Imagine what it would be like to live in a world where people could make little or even a lot of money by simply playing video games. Video games have been one of the most profitable industries of the last decade with stocks like Activision Blizzard (ATVI), Take-Two Interactive (TTWO), and Sea Limited (SE) providing heavy returns to investors. Now, a combination of video games and crypto is set to light a fire under a new wave of profitable investments.

If I asked you to guess what the fastest-growing video game of 2021 was, you would probably say the latest Call of Duty or a viral sensation like Among Us. However, the correct answer might take you by surprise because it is something you might not have heard about: Axie Infinity.

### AXIE INFINITY's *Phenomenal Rise*

Axie Infinity was developed by an obscure Vietnamese developer named Sky Mavis. Axie Infinity is about trading and battling Pokemon-like creatures called Axies, which are Non-Fungible Tokens (NFTs – more on those later), and players are earning thousands of dollars just by playing.

The game has become so popular that within three years, it was valued at over $3 billion after receiving a $152 million funding round from Andreesen Horowitz (Newton, 2021). Nobody knew that playing video games could fetch a meaningful income, which is what made Axie Infinity so well-received and led to the platform's revenue increasing 3000-fold in 2021.

## Detailed revenue per month

| Month - Year | ETH | USD |
|---|---|---|
| 01-2021 | 91.69 | 103,145.39 |
| 02-2021 | 142.34 | 243,665.6 |
| 03-2021 | 379.1 | 656,974.77 |
| 04-2021 | 293.5 | 670,067.48 |
| 05-2021 | 1,049.96 | 2,992,669.28 |
| 06-2021 | 5,446.42 | 12,229,390.23 |
| 07-2021 | 92,004.31 | 196,893,595.19 |
| 08-2021 | 120,547.17 | 364,426,879.93 |
| 09-2021 | 64,933.71 | 220,323,141.38 |
| 10-2021 | 52,652.86 | 196,948,711.87 |
| 11-2021 | 45,559.16 | 202,924,273.6 |

**Figure 7:** Axie Infinity monthly revenue in 2021 (source: AxieWorld)

Previously, we highlighted Skillz (SKLZ) to members of our Capital Gains Multiplier mentorship program. Skillz utilizes a similar play-to-earn concept with fiat currency. Here is an example of how play-to-earn has the ability to change people's lives for the better.

John Aaron Ramos from the Philippines is a 22-year-old who became viral when he shared pictures of his two homes, which he bought from the money earned by playing Axie Infinity. These stories are uplifting because the players are mostly young. Sky Mavis stated that 25% of the players of Axie Infinity never had a bank account before and Axie wallets were the first financial services they were able to access. You can learn about more Axie Infinity stories by watching the short documentary *Play-To-Earn* on YouTube. It's well worth it if you're interested in finding out more about the human side of this project.

From an investor standpoint, managing partners at Andreessen Horowitz feel very hopeful about the concept that Axie Infinity has brought about. According to them, people would love to grab an opportunity that allows them to earn money while enjoying themselves through a game. Axie Infinity is defining a new category, and this mechanism will find itself used repeatedly in future gaming generations.

### THE POTENTIAL BULLISH Thesis

Let me tell you why I am particularly optimistic about cryptocurrencies and blockchain technology in gaming.

At the time of writing, the entire process of playing Axie Infinity is quite complicated. Their website shows an elaborate eight-step process for players to download the game, quite different from a typical onboarding process where you tap 2 buttons and the game installs right in front of you.

Despite the complexity, the game generated more than $1 billion in revenue from in-game transactions in 2021 and became the biggest user of the Ethereum blockchain in the process. What is even more staggering is the company did this with just 600,000 users. Compare that to a traditional video game, Candy Crush, which generated a similar revenue in 2020, yet required 273 million users to do so.

The potential upside is massive, especially as the company just launched its own sidechain (a separate blockchain which runs parallel to Ethereum), which allows players to lower transaction fees by avoiding the main Ethereum blockchain. It is safe to say that cryptos and blockchain make the future of gaming look quite bright.

# BONUS CHAPTER: HOW TO RECOUP THE COST OF THIS BOOK IN LESS THAN 5 MINUTES

I like to overdeliver in these books. So when I discovered a way to do this, I got way too excited and team had to calm me down.

But I'm slipping this bonus chapter in here anyway.

Here's the deal, if you open an account on Coinbase, they will give you $16 worth of cryptocurrency for free (no catches – no minimum deposit or minimum purchase required). Considering that the paperback version of this book has an RRP of $14.95, that means you can recoup the cost of your investment right away.

Here's the step by step guide.

Step 1: Open an account on Coinbase.com (if you already have an account you can do this too!)

Step 2: Click on "Learn and Earn"

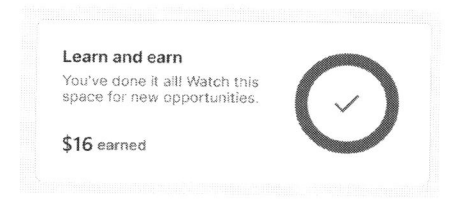

Step 3: Use the following answers for the respective cryptocurrency quizzes

Stellar quiz answers (Reward: $10 worth of XLM)

1. A decentralized protocol that unites the world's financial instruments
2. Facilitating lost-cost universal payments
3. Transactions are fast, inexpensive and global
4. To issue, exchange, and transfer tokens quickly and efficiently
5. It relies on the cooperation of trusted nodes to confirm transactions

AMP quiz answers (Reward: $3 worth of AMP)

1. Collateral Token
2. Instant Settlement Assurance
3. AMP rewards

Fetch quiz answers (Reward: $3 worth of FET)

1. Software agents that automate tasks
2. To power Fetch.ai agents
3. Automated interactions with industries like travel and healthcare

Congratulations, you've now just earned $16 worth of cryptocurrency and made the cost of this book completely free!

And now... back to our regularly scheduled programming.

Oliver

# 6

## THREE SIMPLE WAYS TO PROFIT FROM CRYPTO IN THE STOCK MARKET

Many people who enter the crypto space do so in the hopes of becoming rich overnight. However, if you want to profit long term from crypto, it is important to focus less on the day-to-day swings of Bitcoin and Ethereum and instead look at companies who are set to benefit no matter which coins are surging.

The following 3 stocks are what we call "picks and shovels" plays – because they are directly involved in facilitating cryptocurrency development or transactions, without being having direct involvement with the cryptocurrencies themselves. This investing strategy is named after the tools used to mine for gold during the California Gold Rush. Before prospectors could even find gold, they needed to buy a pick and a shovel so that they could mine for it. So while there was no guarantee that the individual prospector would find gold, the companies that sold picks and shovels were earning revenue regardless.

## Coinbase (COIN)

Coinbase has now become synonymous with cryptocurrencies across the world. Since Coinbase is the biggest and most trusted cryptocurrency exchange, if it were to offer crypto applications through its interface, then most Americans would consequently see these applications as trustworthy.

### BRIEF HISTORY and Development

Founded in July 2012 by former Airbnb engineer Brian Armstrong, Coinbase was first funded by Y Combinator. The creation of Coinbase was a milestone event in the history of the cryptocurrency industry because it was the first medium that was accessible to the general public. It was started as a medium to buy and sell Bitcoin, but today it offers more than 21 products and operates in over 100 countries. It has more than 68 million verified users. This is a huge number in comparison to Wells Fargo, which has 70 million clients, and Bank of America, which has 66 million clients.

### How COINBASE EARNED Its Position

Over the years, Coinbase has played the role of a cryptocurrency kingmaker because of the phenomenal appreciation of the assets listed on the exchange. The boom of the crypto market paired with the excellent services provided by Coinbase in terms of security, ease of use, and regulatory compliance has made it the most important figure in the crypto industry. The company has become an authoritative figure whose stamp of approval is synonymous with authentication.

As a cryptocurrency exchange, Coinbase is of enormous significance because it has made people realize that cryptocurrency is more than a means of exchange and it has real investment value. Coinbase has played an important role in making cryptocurrencies a part of our daily lives by introducing Coinbase cards in the USA, UK, and

EU. This Visa debit card is a crypto wallet that will enable anyone to withdraw cash from the ATM by converting crypto into the desired fiat currency. Cryptocurrency exchanges have been notorious for being hacked due to a general lack of security. Coinbase has always been a step ahead in this regard because they hold and insure all the assets held by them. It stores most of the crypto assets in offline cold storage vaults so that the risk of hacking is reduced and the remaining assets are insured by Lloyd's of London. The American users' funds in USD wallets are covered by the FDIC and insured up to $250,000. Coinbase ensures to provide a secure trading platform to all its users, which is what has made it a commercially successful company with solid profit margins.

### What Are the Possible Hurdles?

Despite the many benefits of Coinbase, it is not free from its share of hurdles. The company has been actively engaging with SEC about their lending program called Lend, which would enable the users to lend the USDC that they hold on the Coinbase platform. The SEC refuses to approve the program by stating that Lend is classified as an "investment contract" rather than a traditional lending program, which means they believe there is an inherent risk on the part of the borrower. However, Coinbase argues that the customers will earn interest from their participation, which will be paid regardless of the broader business objectives of the company. These regulatory hurdles become a greater problem since other crypto companies have been running lending programs for years without seeking approval from the SEC. Moreover, with time Coinbase and Coinbase Pro are facing stiff competition from other crypto-asset exchanges like Bitfinex, Bitstamp, and Kraken.

### Understanding the Future and the Risks Associated with Investing in Coinbase Stock

Coinbase has always believed in bringing economic freedom to the users of cryptocurrencies. They were the first website to simplify buying and selling cryptocurrencies, and they intend to do the same with NFTs. Coinbase has announced its NFT with the aim of minting, purchasing, and trading NFTs with ease.

The company has always been a trendsetter and continued to do so when they opted for a direct listing on the NASDAQ exchange instead of an IPO. This non-traditional yet trendy choice was apt for Coinbase since they have been the pioneers of non-traditional cryptocurrencies for the last decade. However, there are certain inherent risks associated with the Coinbase stock, in case you are thinking of investing.

The company is heavily dependent on retail cryptocurrency trading, which comprises 82% of its total revenue. If you add institutional trading to that, 87% of the company's total revenue will be dependent on cryptocurrency trading volumes, which have historically been very volatile (Sigalos, 2021).

WHAT'S MORE IS, the price of the stock moves in line with the price of Bitcoin itself, as it is the most dominant coin on the market.

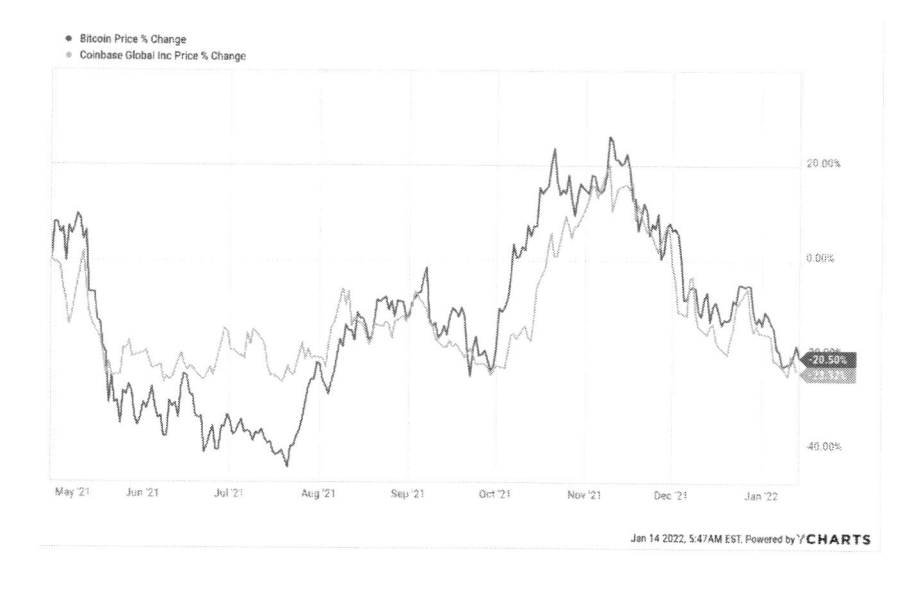

**Figure 8:** The heavy correlation between the price of Coinbase stock and the price of Bitcoin itself (Source: Ycharts)

ANOTHER FACTOR AFFECTING Coinbase going forward is the continued competition in the cryptocurrency exchange market. At the time of writing, Coinbase's market cap of $49 billion is around 2% of the total market cap of all cryptocurrencies. Compared to another brokerage stock in Charles Schwab which is around 0.38% the market cap of total US equities. Alternatively, you could compare it to Nasdaq, whose stock is roughly 0.07% of total US equities. So while the cryptocurrency market will inevitably increase in size over the next decade, I would not expect Coinbase stock to keep pace with it.

Due to the recent pullback, Coinbase stock is trading relatively cheaply (6.5x 2022 sales) compared to both Nasdaq (10.8x 2022 sales) and NYSE owner Intercontinental Exchange (9.8x 2022 sales).

You can expect Coinbase to stay very unstable over the next 12 to

18 months but if you can build a position starting at a stock price below \$220, then you will be setup nicely for the years to come.

## Silvergate Capital Corporation (SI)

For generations, finance and trading have always been associated with banks. The advent of cryptocurrencies and blockchains challenged this tradition by developing a decentralized network. However, that does not change the fact that people still feel comparatively safer when a bank is involved. Silvergate Capital Corporation understood this and grabbed the opportunity to become the first crypto bank in the world. It has been a long-standing player in the financial market and has remained profitable for the past 21 years. It provides financial infrastructure services to the participants of the digital currency space.

This relatively small crypto bank looks strong and shows ample promise for growth across multiple digital currencies including stablecoins. In simpler terms, it is a custodian of crypto assets in addition to offering normal banking services. It provides collateralized lending of Bitcoin, which is growing at a staggering rate of 25% per quarter.

### *Silvergate Exchange Network (SEN)*

In 2017, the company wanted to target the unexplored digital currency network, which was why they introduced the Silvergate Exchange Network (SEN). Investors were overwhelmed due to the 24/7 trading hours of cryptocurrencies and were facing major problems in sending funds across various platforms because the trading timings varied from the normal banking hours. Silvergate Capital Corporation addressed this problem by developing the first API-enabled real-time payment platform called SEN. Since SEN is a two-sided network, it allows its members to conduct transactions all year round on a real-time basis. This created a huge competitive advantage for both the users and participating networks, which attracted more people and exchanges to become a part of the cryptocurrency space. SEN provides interest-free deposits and cross-sells additional services by capitalizing its first-mover advantage which is contributing to its rapid growth. SEN is regarded as the core of the Silvergate Capital Corporation and is now recognized as an industry-leading payment network utilized by major crypto exchanges and institutional investors.

### Opportunities in Lending *and Stablecoins*

With the increased popularity of crypto lending, SI launched SEN Leverage, which allows users to get loans collateralized by bitcoins which are held at specified exchanges. Their network allows them to process loans and repayments any time of the day. They have associated themselves with Bitstamp Ltd to manage the cryptocurrency collaterals. Although it is a relatively new part of SI, SEN has shown rapid growth by becoming 16% of their entire loan portfolio in comparison to 2% of the previous year (Analyst, 2021). As a user, you get the benefit of flexibility and security since SEN maintains a loan-to-value ratio of 50-65% and handles volatile cryptocurrencies by enforcing various risk control measures.

Stablecoin opportunities can become beneficial for SI as Meta Platforms (formerly Facebook) has announced a partnership with them. SI will be the exclusive manager and issuer of the Diem USD stablecoin which will be introduced by Facebook. The Diem network will include many high-profile customers like Coinbase, Uber, Lyft, Farfetch, and Spotify. SI's association with Diem can mean increased income and profits through transaction fees and income on reserve deposits.

### The Future Prospects

SEN is a particularly successful segment since it has incurred zero losses and there have been no forced liquidations to date. The company ended the quarter with 1,305 digital currency customers, up from 928 in the third quarter of 2020 and 1,224 in the second quarter of 2021. The transfer volume on SEN reached $219 billion in Q4 of 2021, from which Silvergate was able to generate $9.3 million in transaction fees (Silvergate Capital, 2022).

However, you must not let the recent run-up fool you since this is still at a very early stage at just a $3.5 billion market cap. In March 2021, SI announced its association with Fidelity Digital Assets as their custody provider. This was a huge milestone for them since this would mean that institutional investors would be able to receive USD financing using the SEN and the collateral (the Bitcoin) will be held by Fidelity Digital Assets separately in a cold storage account. Silvergate Capital Corporation also announced partnerships with major companies like PayPal and CME Group. It provides a moving line of credit of $100 million to Marathon Digital, which makes it a good acquisition target for big banks, such as, J.P. Morgan.

In terms of valuation, SI shows the potential of a quintessential growth stock with a forward price-earnings ratio of 36 and a forward price-sales ratio of 14. The leadership position and value of the SEN as a fintech platform justifies the bullish valuation.

### Blockchain Exchange Traded Funds (ETFs)

The blockchain market has a compound annual growth rate of 50% since it is still in the early stages of development. If you aren't comfortable with investing in individual stocks, then Blockchain ETFs offer an efficient investment opportunity to put your money in a basket of stocks that specifically deal with blockchains.

#### GLOBAL X BLOCKCHAIN ETF (BKCH)

The Global X Blockchain ETF (BKCH) invests in companies that are set to benefit from blockchain adoption in their business operations. They also invest in companies involved in digital asset mining, digital asset hardware, and blockchain digital asset integration. It has a net expense ratio of 0.5%. This fund is more mining and crypto-exchange focused and is heavily concentrated since almost 55% of the fund is invested in Coinbase, Marathon Digital, Hut 8 Mining, Riot Blockchain and Voyager Digital. BKCH is more volatile than the other Blockchain ETFs discussed because the prices of mining stocks have a high correlation with Bitcoin prices.

### Amplified Transformational Data *Sharing ETF (BLOK)*

The fund has been around since 2018 and the majority of its holdings are in software which implies that it is more fintech related. As of September 30, 2021, the top five companies in which this fund has invested are Hut 8 Corporation, MicroStrategy, Block (formerly known as Square), PayPal, and Marathon Digital Holdings Inc. The fund has a net expense ratio of 0.71%.

### *Invesco CoinShares Global Blockchain UCITS ETF (BCHS)*

For our readers in the UK and EU, the best European Blockchain ETF is BCHS. This ETF is listed in London and has over 1 billion GBP in assets under management. The fund has a net expense ratio of 0.65% and the top 10 holdings include as mixture of both mining focused companies and FinTech companies like Hive Blockchain Technologies, Bitfarms Ltd, SBI Holdings Inc, Coinbase Global Inc, Taiwan Semiconductor Manufacturing, GMO Internet Inc, Monex Group Inc, Microstrategy Inc, and Kakao Corp.

# 7

# TWO WAYS TO NOT GET EXPOSURE TO CRYPTO IN THE STOCK MARKET + ONE WAY WE'RE RECONSIDERING

C rypto enthusiasts will keep telling you all the things that you *should* do to become a millionaire in this market. However, there is no denying the fact that this market changes colors frequently and it is very difficult to predict anything with reasonable certainty.

Our suggestion has always been very straightforward: invest in crypto only if you feel you have the stomach for it and don't let the fear of missing out drive your decisions. Just because the media or some tech-bloggers are hyping something does not mean you have to put all your money into it. The crypto market is deceiving, which is why you should steer clear of these three things when you decide to become a part of this space.

**ProShares Bitcoin Strategy ETF (BITO)**

After years of battling back and forth with the SEC to get regulatory approval, October 2021 saw the launch of the first-ever Bitcoin ETF located in the USA with the ProShares Bitcoin Strategy ETF (BITO) hitting the exchanges. This was an achievement in itself because this was the first time in around eight years that a cryptocurrency proponent was able to secure a badge of legitimacy and authentication from the Securities Exchange Commission (SEC). It was the fastest ETF ever to reach $1 billion assets under management (AUM) by achieving this milestone within a day of its launch.

### Why this ETF isn't what it first appears

The investment policy of the ProShares ETF mentions that its main objective is to achieve capital appreciation, by investing in Bitcoin futures contracts. This means that the fund does not directly invest in Bitcoin, nor does it track the spot price of Bitcoin.

Therefore owning BITO is not like GLD, which provides ownership of gold by proxy. Since the fund is giving you exposure to Bitcoin futures, the current price may not reflect the spot price of Bitcoin. The ETF puts their money in cash-settled, front-month Bitcoin futures. Front-month means contracts whose maturity dates are the soonest. At the end of the month, the ETF will roll their Bitcoin futures over to the next month. They can do this by selling the contracts of the current month and again buying contracts for next month. This process continues, and as the price of futures changes, the value of the ETF fluctuates. This process is known as "rolling yield."

Here's where the problem lies: shorter-term traders know that the ETF has to roll over its contracts, which is why these traders drive up the price of the coming month's contracts. As a result, BITO is forced to pay a higher price for next month's futures.

THE ROLLING YIELD method is a direct impact of the constant state of Contango of the Bitcoin futures market. Contango is a situation where the price of futures keeps on increasing as time passes, which means the fund has to sell the expiring futures at a lower price while buying new futures at a much higher price. BITO already accounts for one third of the Bitcoin futures market, and it will only increase as time passes and more institutional investment goes into the fund.

Because of this, the ETF will be paying an 8-10% higher price for the fresh futures, which implies that you will be getting only $0.90 worth of Bitcoin for every $1 invested in the ETF. Moreover, future prices are based on prevailing spot prices plus the cost of carry, which may be positive or negative depending on the demand and supply forces. This makes the prices of the ETF unstable and might create problems for the investor.

### Bitwise 10 Crypto Index Fund (BITW)

Bitwise Asset Management is the world's largest crypto index fund manager, which introduced the Bitwise 10 Crypto Index Fund. It describes itself as something similar to the "S&P 500 of Crypto." This is supposed to be the first large-cap crypto index fund that exposes the investor to the so-called "exciting" world of crypto beyond Bitcoin. It is another one of those "Bitcoin fund" type of deals and holds 84% Bitcoin and 11% Ethereum. The remaining 5% is invested in 7 different cryptocurrencies like Litecoin, Solana, Uniswap, and Chainlink.

DESPITE THE HIGH claims made by the fund, it does not perform. I say this because the fund has an insanely high expense ratio of 2.5%. Funds that seek to correspond to the S&P 500 Index have expense ratios that range from only 0.015% to 0.09%, which is why it is quite evident that this comparison is completely unjustified.

ANOTHER ISSUE with these funds is that they trade only Monday to Friday. They have not yet reached the level of dynamism of crypto trading that is taking place 24/7. This is an issue because of the associated volatility that comes with investing in the crypto market. Imagine there is a major drop in Bitcoin prices over the weekend. What happens to your investment in the BITW fund? You are left exposed because you won't be able to makes any trades until the following Monday.

### Grayscale Bitcoin Trust (GBTC)

GBTC rose to popularity in 2020 as it was the most liquid way to get exposure to Bitcoin in a traditional retirement account like an IRA, Roth IRA or 401(k). We previously discussed GBTC in our book *The Only Bitcoin Investing Book You'll Ever Need*.

In that book, we discouraged readers from investing due to the high management fee and the fact that the fund was trading at a significant premium in relation to its Net Asset Value (NAV). However, since then, we have seen an interesting phenomenon with GBTC.

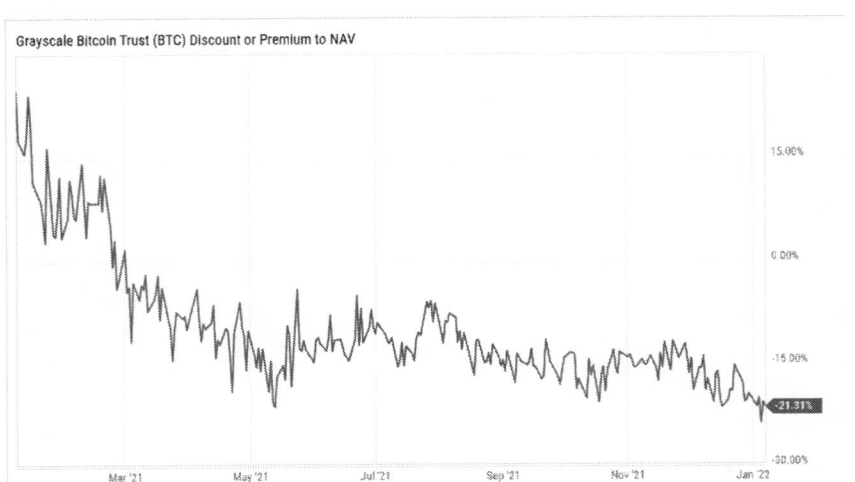

**Figure 9:** GBTC swings from a heavy premium to a significant discount to NAV (Source: YCharts)

As you can see, the fund spent the majority of 2021 (and continues into 2022) trading at a large discount to NAV. Meaning instead of paying $1.20 for $1 worth of Bitcoin like you would have done at the beginning of 2021, at the time of writing you could buy Bitcoin for 79 cents on the dollar.

We still recommend direct Bitcoin ownership over everything else, but if you do want exposure to Bitcoin in your retirement account, then GBTC is worth buying *only* if the fund is trading at a significant discount to NAV.

# 8

# WHAT THE "F" IS AN NFT?

The rise of the digital world has given a twist to the art and collectibles industry. That's right, blockchain has penetrated the world of art and collectibles as well, and right now we've seen a new wave of cryptoassets come to the forefront. Let me introduce you to the world of non-fungible tokens, or NFTs.

## Deconstructing NFTs

If you're unfamiliar, then NFTs can seem confusing or downright bizarre. Are people paying $100,000 for a JPEG image? Can't you just copy that same image on your computer? Did Snoop Dogg really spend $17m on NFTs under the pseudonym Cozomo De Medici?

The answer to that last one is, indeed, yes. You can see Snoop Dogg's NFT portfolio by going to

HTTPS://FREEMANPUBLICATIONS.COM/SNOOPDOGGWALLET

**Figure 10:** Cryptopunk #3100, an NFT which sold for 4,200 ETH ($7.58m) in March 2021

### So what exactly IS an NFT?

An NFT, or Non-Fungible Token, is a form of a digital asset that represents things like art, music, in-game objects, and videos. They have the same underlying technology as cryptocurrencies—that is, blockchain. NFTs have been around since 2014, but they have suddenly started gaining popularity for buying and selling digital artwork. Over $174 million has been spent on NFTs since 2017 (Conti, 2021).

CONNOISSEURS, celebrities and speculators want access to something exclusive and to claim ownership over a piece of art that will not be replicated anytime soon. The NFT craze is not just limited to art. Remember those sports cards you used to collect as a child? They have now become digital and are represented as sports moments with movement and sound, and each of them is one of a kind. This uniqueness is making collectors reach deep into their pockets to pull out millions of dollars without a second thought.

.   .   .

YOU MIGHT BE WONDERING, what is so special about a sports clip? The same clip is being edited millions of times on all social media platforms. People are making TikTok videos, reels, and whatnot with those clips, so why would somebody want to spend a fortune for it? Well, it might not make sense for you, but a crazy sports fan would take pride in owning the "original" clip. These NFTs give the owner a kind of digital bragging rights, and for some people, that is worth a lot.

### How Do NFTs Differ From Traditional Cryptocurrencies?

THE CRYPTO WORLD has two types of tokens, which are fungible and non-fungible. All digital currencies are fungible tokens like physical money. This means that the value of one bitcoin will always be equal to another. Even if it is converted to dollars, the value will remain unchanged.

NON-FUNGIBLE TOKENS ARE unique and one token cannot be exchanged for one another. For example, Mike Winklemann, the famous digital artist also known as Beeple, crafted 5,000 daily drawings to create one of the most famous NFTs of the moment. Known as "Everydays: The First 5000 Days," it was sold at $69.3 million (Copeland, 2021). An NBA Top Shot of LeBron James sold for $250,000. These two NFTs are different and there cannot be any exchange between the two.

### How Do NFTs Work?

Like cryptocurrencies, blockchain is the central technology of NFTs. Although many other networks support them, NFTs are most commonly found on the Ethereum blockchain. These tokens are created or "minted" from digital objects, which may represent art,

GIFs, sports highlights, collectibles, video game skins, virtual avatars, designer sneakers, music, and any other tangible or intangible item. An NFT is not much different from buying a painting from an art gallery. Instead of hanging it in your living room, you get a digital file with the original artwork or collectible. Their ownership is verified with the help of a unique digital signature, which is proof of authenticity.

### WHAT ARE the Uses of NFTs?

Artists have always had a hard time finding buyers for their art through galleries or auction houses. Often, they do not get the price they are looking for. Even if they do find a suitable buyer, much of the profit gets eaten up by intermediaries.

NFTs REMOVE this barrier because they connect the artist directly with the consumer. We are not here to talk just about art, which is why it is important to understand the benefits NFTs provide for investors as well. The removal of intermediaries enables a buyer to pay the right price for their desired piece of art. Moreover, NFTs have created a demand for some strange yet impactful things.

POPULAR BRANDS LIKE TACO BELL, Coca-Cola and Charmin have used NFTs to raise money for charity. These tokens improve market efficiency by easily converting a physical item to a digital asset and assigning a suitable value to it.

IF USED CORRECTLY, NFTs have the potential to revolutionize complex investments like real estate. Division of property can become much easier by assigning an NFT of each part of the property to every owner. Decentraland is a virtual reality platform on the Ethereum network which has implemented a similar concept. It is assumed that as NFTs become more developed, we will be able to implement the concept of tokenized pieces of land to physical real estate as well based on their value and location.

### Understanding the Value of NFTs

The biggest reason why certain NFTs are so valuable is because of their scarcity. Imagine waiting in line for a long time to buy something exclusive. NFTs are simply the digital version of that same event. As with many other collectibles, the value of NFTs is linked to their scarcity. There is only one original version of the *Mona Lisa*, and if you wish to own it, you will have to pay its price. NFTs derive their value from a similar logic. Because they are rare or unique, they are often valued at millions of dollars. Except, unlike physical art which is often replicated or faked, because of the underlying records stored on the blockchain, it is impossible to fake or duplicate an NFT because of their immutable transaction history.

### The Four Components *of NFT Value*

Scarcity cannot be considered as the only factor while determining the value of NFTs, which is why the following formula is often used to understand and deconstruct their value. Depending on which asset the NFT represents, the following elements are used by the investors to figure out whether the token is worth spending money for. Creators also consider these elements to check whether there is scope for increasing the value.

**Value of an NFT = Utility + Ownership History + Future Value + Liquidity Premium**

### Utility

The utility is one of the biggest indicators of determining the value for any asset, and NFTs are no exception. Two of the most popular items that determine utility in the world of NFTs are tickets and game assets. A powerful and rare Crypto Space Battleship token was sold for $45,250 in 2019 (Chang, 2020). This is also why Axie Infinity has taken off so much, because each Axie character functions as its own NFT, and as the Axie gains more powers within the game, it increases in value.

. . .

ANOTHER WAY TO determine the utility of an NFT is determining whether this token can be used in any other application. Although the chances of this happening are quite rare because there is an inherent lack of interoperability, if the space battleship could be used in another game, then its value would be high. It must be noted that multiple applications do not signify exchange like a fungible token. Right now, the NFT space is dominated by a few games, and to make the tokens universally acceptable, a massive ecosystem needs to be developed.

## OWNERSHIP HISTORY

The identity of the creator or issuer and previous owners of the NFT play a very important role in determining its value. Digital art creators can consider partnering with companies with a high brand value to issue their tokens since a high ownership history is instrumental in increasing the price of the token. The value of the NFT might also increase if it was previously owned by somebody influential. Various marketplaces and trading platforms allow users and investors to track individuals who have made the most profit using NFTs.

## FUTURE VALUE

The future value of an NFT has two components: valuation changes and future cash flow. Since the financial market is highly driven by speculation right now, the future value can change drastically within a short span, which can become the main driver for the valuation of the NFT. Scarcity and speculation can drive NFT prices like nothing else, which is what makes it one of the most important determinants of their value.

## LIQUIDITY PREMIUM

On-chain NFTs offer greater liquidity than off-chain ones. For example, if an NFT is available on the Ethereum network, anyone holding Ether can easily trade in those NFTs and their risk of liquidity will be significantly reduced. That is why investors like to invest in NFTs that have a high trading value.

Apart from all these factors, another important point that determines the value of NFTs is the individual investor's perception. For example, for a crazy basketball fan, a clip of LeBron James dunking NBA Top Shots might be priceless, which can drive them to pay a very high amount for a so-called "useless" asset.

**Sneaky Ways to Profit From the Boom of NFTs**

NFTs are still at their early stages, which is why there is a lot of speculation in this sector. Like we keep saying, just because everyone else is doing it doesn't mean you have to spend money on NFTs as well. Our suggestion is to not buy the NFTs themselves if you are not into collecting rare and collectible items. The big meme NFTs like Crypto Kitties or Cyberpunks are highly manipulated, which is why you might end up buying something worthless. Since the space is still relatively new, you have to do your research to understand the profit element in them.

*EARNING From NFTs if You Are a Creator*

For creators, NFTs are a great way to showcase their art to a bigger audience. When Beeple's painting collage made a record at Christie's by selling at $69.3 million, the whole world understood that NFTs can mean something huge for creators of digital art. Many people believe that paying millions for a link to a picture is nothing but a scam, but the consensus is that NFTs will revolutionize the whole art space.

CREATORS OF SPORTS cards can also earn a fortune by selling their NFTs. Sports cards have always been extremely popular among their collectors, but physical cards have the risk of getting destroyed. NFTs eliminate any such risks by tokenizing the cards. Not just sports cards, creators of any rare collectibles can create their NFTs and sell them on the digital marketplace.

Companies involved in developing games have their eyes set on NFTs after the phenomenal success of Axie Infinity. Gamers are famous for spending recklessly while playing, which is why the gaming industry can benefit a lot from NFTs. World of Warcraft gold or Call of Duty loot boxes and other video game skins are already worth billions of dollars, and if any game thinks about selling in-game items as NFTs, it could boost their income tremendously (Leyes, 2021).

## TRADING NFTS

Although we do not recommend trading directly in NFTs due to the inherent risks involved, you can give it a try if you feel you have enough knowledge about artsy collectibles and how this market works. A Miami-based art collector named Pablo Rodriguez-Fraile sold a digital art piece by Beeple for almost 1,000 times its initial price (Fintelics, 2021). The value of NFTs varies significantly, which means among two similar art pieces, one can be worth millions and another completely worthless. This makes direct trading of NFTs difficult and unpredictable.

## EARNING Passive Income From NFTs

If you are someone who has purchased an NFT on the spur of the moment and now don't know what to do with it, here are a few ways through which you can earn passive income from them:

- **Renting Out NFTs:** Many card trading games give the option of borrowing NFTs to increase their chances of winning. These agreements are governed by smart contracts which will keep you safe when you rent your NFTs. You will be allowed to set the rental agreement, including lease rate and duration, so the whole deal stays under your control.

- **Royalties:** As the creator of an NFT, you can mint it in such a way that it gives you a fixed percentage of royalty every time it is sold in the secondary market. Smart contracts control the entire process and you don't have to worry about asking for royalties.
- **Staking NFTs:** The combination of NFTs with decentralized finance allows you to "stake" your purchased NFTs, which is a process of locking your tokens and earning a subsequent yield from them with the help of a DeFi protocol smart contract.
- **Providing Liquidity:** Decentralized finance gives you the option to provide liquidity by using your NFTs.

### *Where Can You Trade NFTs?*

The first step would be to have a cryptocurrency wallet through which the transactions will take place. The good news is that because the vast majority of NFTs are on the Ethereum blockchain, then any wallet with Ethereum compatibility will suffice.

The most NFT friendly wallet is Metamask, which comes with features like a browser extension and the ability to set up multiple addresses. The latter is useful if you would like to hold your NFTs in a separate wallet from your regular crypto holdings.

WE HAVE a video tutorial on setting up your Metamask wallet at https://freemanpublications.com/cryptotutorials

MOST NFT TRADES TAKE place using cryptocurrency (usually Ethereum), so you would need the required currency as well. These are the most popular digital marketplaces that facilitate buying and selling of NFTs:

- **Open Sea.io:** This is a digital platform that hosts a collection of rare items, and you can easily access them by creating an account. You can also find popular artists by filtering by their sales volume.
- **Rarible:** This platform uses Rari tokens for fees and other community rules. Rarible is a democratic platform where you can easily access and trade NFTs.
- **Foundation:** This is more of an exclusive platform where artists can only post their art after receiving an invitation from a collector. These invitations are called "upvotes." Foundation has a high entry cost since artists have to purchase "gas" to mint NFTs. This is a premium platform attracting collectors who can pay very high prices. Chris Torres sold the famous Nyan Cat NFT through Foundation.
- **NFT-Specific Marketplaces:** Certain NFTs trade directly on their own platforms like NBA TopShot, Larva Labs (CryptoPunks) and Axie Marketplace.

## Understand the Risks and Invest in the Platforms

The barriers to entry in the NFT market are extremely low. Anybody can create an NFT and obtain a digital certificate for it, which is why it is necessary to consider the following risk factors before investing in NFTs:

- NFTs might be subject to copyright issues. Anybody can create a digital token from an asset, after which they are assigned a digital signature which acts as a verification. However, this digital key is not a guarantee of initial ownership, which is what raises a question about their genuineness.
- No formal rules and regulations are governing NFTs, which is why their price can change at the whim of the manipulators. OpenSea issued a statement stating that

one of their employees purchased NFTs knowing that they would be featured on OpenSea's front page. After they were published, the prices of the NFTs were boosted and they sold them at a high profit. This shows the amount of unregulated manipulation that exists in this market.

Since NFTs are still in a nascent phase, we recommend against trying to make money by trading NFTs themselves. We preferred a picks and shovels approach where we invest in platforms like Solana and Polkadot that facilitate the sale of NFTs, rather than the NFTs directly.

*OUTSIDE SHOT*
Sports-related NFTs are extremely popular in this market, which is why an under-the-radar play is to buy stocks from sports teams with an NFT angle.

SUPPOSE an NFT is created by Manchester United featuring Cristiano Ronaldo scoring the winning goal in a cup final. There won't be any question about its rising values, and subsequently, the club to which the player belongs will also profit from this NFT.

THAT IS why you can consider investing in stocks like Madison Square Garden (MSGE), Liberty Global (LBTY), Manchester United (LSE:MANU), and Juventus (BIT:JUVE). In this way, you will be able to get exposure to NFTs without suffering from their volatility directly.

DESPITE THE BUZZ AROUND NFTs, it is still early to comment on their long-term viability right now. If used properly, they have the potential to become a good virtual twin for a digital asset, especially in sectors like real estate, by easing the trading process, allowing simple divisions, and tracing its history and ownership.

REMEMBER though that this is a highly speculative and volatile market, and that fundamental, technical, or economic factors often fail to impact NFT prices because everything is dependent upon demand. Before investing, you should always consider the resale options. An NFT might not fetch any value on resale if nobody wants it during the time you want to sell it, which makes it a bit dysfunctional as an investment. Conduct thorough research and understand your priorities before making a decision.

# 9

## FREQUENTLY ASKED QUESTIONS FROM FIRST-TIME CRYPTO INVESTORS

There is still a lot of gray area in the cryptocurrency market. The majority of countries have yet to develop proper laws for regulating crypto. Naturally, there is a lot of doubt about how to proceed with your investments and what the implications will be. That is why in this chapter we will address some of the frequently asked questions from first-time crypto investors, especially concerning its taxation and future planning. Even if you have invested in crypto before, the answers to these questions will come in handy when you are stuck.

### Can I Own Bitcoin/Ethereum in My IRA?

Investing in cryptocurrencies as a part of your retirement portfolio can be a good idea since it might result in substantially higher returns. You have the option of investing in cryptos through a self-directed IRA because normal IRAs do not allow you to put your money in alternative assets.

The money that you deposit in this self-directed IRA will be invested to purchase cryptocurrencies instead of normal mutual funds. For a Bitcoin IRA, you have to remember that a custodian like a bank or a financial institution ensures that your account is following the relevant rules and regulations.

The biggest advantage of a Bitcoin IRA is that you get the benefit of diversification since the value of cryptocurrencies is not linked with stocks. Even if the stock market is going down, you have the chance to earn phenomenally high returns. Both Bitcoin and Ethereum have shown huge growth over the last couple of years, and they are expected to continue this trend. Investing in a Bitcoin IRA gives you tax benefits like a normal IRA.

If you decide to open a Bitcoin IRA, here are a few leading providers which will allow you to choose from a variety of cryptocurrencies to invest in:

- BitIRA
- Bitcoin IRA
- Equity Trust
- iTrustCapital
- Regal Assets (if you want to own more cryptocurrencies beyond just Bitcoin)

Please do your due diligence before converting anything over to a Bitcoin or Crypto IRA. Especially be sure to take note of all fees associated with setting up and maintaining the account. Self directed IRAs can be time consuming and expensive to set up (and even more so if you do things incorrectly). This is not a financial decision that you want to make on a whim.

### Can I Own Cryptocurrency in a 401(k) Account?

Technically, it is possible, but if you are under an employer-sponsored 401(k) plan, you will not be allowed to put that money in cryptocurrencies. This is because employer-sponsored plans are covered by the ERISA fiduciary rules, which protect the investors from the volatility of large losses. Since the primary objective of a 401(k) account is to save money for retirement, the ERISA fiduciary rules ensure that the money in this account is kept safe.

However, if you are a self-employed person sponsoring your retirement through a Solo 401(k), you can choose to invest a part of it in cryptocurrencies.

## Questions Regarding Taxability of Cryptocurrencies

First of all, I would like to clarify that we are not tax professionals. We are here to talk about cryptocurrencies and are not providing tax advice. We recommend that you consult your local professional when you are filing your tax returns because there may be certain issues that are specific to you. There is still huge confusion about the taxability of cryptocurrencies. Cryptocurrencies are yet to receive the status of "medium of exchange," so they are not taxed in the exact same way as stocks are.

### Do I Have to Pay Taxes on My Crypto Gains?

Yes, you do. The IRS (and HMRC in the UK) treats capital gains on cryptocurrency the same way they treat stocks. They are considered as personal assets of the holder. When you sell cryptocurrencies, you have to pay capital gains on the amount of profit that you earned. Gambling wins are exempt from tax in the UK, but cryptocurrency transactions are not considered gambling, which is why you must pay taxes on the gains. It is not considered a currency since it is not issued by any central bank. If you are holding crypto for less than 365 days, you will have to pay short-term taxes on the gains. Long-term capital gains will be taxed if you are holding the currencies for a longer period.

### WHICH CRYPTO TRANSACTIONS ARE TAXED?

The IRS considers the following transactions related to cryptocurrencies as taxable:

- Selling cryptocurrency which you have personally mined to a third party. If you have mined cryptocurrency and sold it to a third party for a profit, then that profit will be liable for capital gain taxes.
- Selling cryptocurrency to a third party which you have purchased. If you have bought cryptocurrencies from an exchange and sold them to a third party for a profit, then you will be paying capital gains taxes on it.
- Buying goods or services with cryptocurrency which you have mined. For example, if you purchased a pizza using cryptocurrency that you mined, then that transaction will attract capital gains taxes. The amount of taxes will depend on the nature of the transaction and the value of cryptocurrency in comparison to that of the pizza.
- Buying goods and services with cryptocurrency which you have bought. If you purchased cryptocurrencies from an exchange and subsequently used the same for buying some goods or services, such a transaction will attract capital gain taxes.

In the second and fourth scenarios, it is a lot like investing in an asset. However, for the cases where you are mining the cryptocurrency, you may be able to get deductions for any expenses which you have incurred during the mining process.

### DOES a Cryptocurrency Miner Have to Pay Taxes?

As mentioned above, the mining of cryptocurrencies is a taxable event and the fair market value will be the current value of the currency at the time of being mined. If you are in the business of cryptocurrency mining, then you can claim the expenses that you have incurred like resources, software and save big bucks on your taxes. However, if you have mined the coins for personal benefit, you will not be getting any deduction.

### ARE CRYPTOCURRENCY CONVERSIONS TAXED?

Conversions between Bitcoin and Ether, or between any other currencies, were considered as a like-kind transfer and income tax on such transactions could be deferred as per the permissions of the IRS.

However, the IRS put a stop to it after they found rampant exploitations of this provision. It was stated by the Tax Cuts and Jobs Act of 2017 that like-kind transactions could take place only in real estate.

However, if you transfer cryptocurrency from one wallet to another, it will <u>not</u> be considered a sale and hence no capital gains will be attracted.

### WHAT HAPPENS When There Is a Hard Fork in the Blockchain?

A hard fork is an incident when a blockchain undergoes a protocol change and the old cryptocurrencies on the network are dropped. A new coin is created which is different from its predecessor in mining and features. Holders of the original cryptocurrency may be allotted new coins, and this phenomenon is called an airdrop. IRS clarified that there are no tax implications of a hard fork, but when the holder receives units of a new cryptocurrency, it results in gross income and is subsequently taxed as normal income.

### What Happens When I Donate, Gift, or Inherit Cryptocurrencies?

The donation of crypto is treated the same way as cash donations. The amount of gain as calculated by an appraiser during the time of donation will not attract any tax.

Gifts of cryptocurrencies below $15,000 are not subject to tax but will be taxed once this limit is exceeded. Inheritance of cryptocurrency is treated the same way as other estate assets.

### Filing and Reducing Crypto Taxes

In our years of academic and practical experience, we have gathered knowledge about the tax filing process, which we are sharing with you. Please consult your tax advisor regarding your particular tax situation.

- **Keep a record of all transactions:** The IRS has made it mandatory for every person to keep a record of cryptocurrency transactions. This will include details of your purchases, how long you have held the currencies, and records of every transaction where you used crypto to buy any goods or services. Your crypto exchange will provide a 1099-B form to both you and the IRS as a report of your transactions, but this might not include the transactions you made between offline cold wallets. You can use the help of software packages like Koinly or Cointracker, which help you to track all your cryptocurrency transactions across all blockchains, even if they are not on the network.
- **Fill out the proper forms:** If you are making transactions

in cryptocurrencies, you must fill out the correct forms to avoid penalties. Depending on how you are using crypto, there are various forms to fill. Form 8949 logs crypto as an investment where you have to enter the number of coins held, date and price of purchase and sale, and the amount of loss and gain. Schedule D will summarize all your capital gains, including ones from crypto. If you have mined cryptocurrencies, you have to disclose details in Schedule C. In case you have mined coins as a hobby, you have to disclose that in Schedule 1.

- **File your taxes:** Using a software package like Koinly or Cointracker will help you to keep track of all the transactions, and then you can link this record to your main federal and state tax form. You can also choose to opt for a package like TokenTax, which is an integrated solution for both your cryptocurrency and regular taxes. They will provide you with assistance with the entire thing.

If all these discussions about taxes are making you anxious, don't worry. Here are a few ways through which you can save on cryptocurrency taxes in the future:

- Holding your cryptocurrencies for a longer term will help you save a lot on taxes. Depending on how much you have earned during the year, your short-term capital gains rate is around 37% while your long-term rate will be lower. So just by retaining the investments for a longer period, you can cut your tax rate significantly.
- The main reason why people hold cryptocurrency investments is to take advantage of the volatility and cash in profits when the market is at a high. If you are thinking about selling a huge chunk of your holdings for profit, take a look at your other investments and see if you are incurring heavy losses in any of them. If your other

holdings (whether crypto or not) are at a loss, then you can sell those during the same year to offset the gains from your crypto investment sale.

- When you invest in crypto funds or ETFs through retirement accounts like self-directed IRA or 401(k), you get the benefits of tax deferment

# 10

# COMMON CRYPTO SCAMS TO WATCH OUT FOR

W henever something new pops up, there are always bad actors snooping around to make a quick buck. Along with all the good investment, this industry has also become home to a variety of fraudsters and scammers. According to the Federal Trade Commission (FTC) Consumer Sentinel, from October 2020 through March 31, 2021, reports of crypto-related scams skyrocketed to nearly 7,000 people reporting losses of more than $80 million.

THESE FIGURES REFLECT a 12-fold increase in the number of reports compared to the same period a year ago and a nearly 1,000% rise in reported losses (Liebkind, 2021). In this chapter, we will talk about the various scams that the cryptocurrency industry is seeing so that you don't fall prey to them.

## Use of Authority Figures and Pop Culture

One trend which I have been noticing in the past few months is that people who used to sell real estate seminars or forex seminars have suddenly become "experts in cryptocurrencies" and are more than eager to show you how much they have gained in the last two or three months. If you have come across such people, take a thousand steps back from them and think about the big picture. Look for people who have been doing this for years, not months. People are always jumping on the bandwagon, which is why you will find 20-year-old kids who have made a couple of trades turning into self-proclaimed gurus. Here are two such very common methods of scamming people in the crypto market:

*USE OF AUTHORITY Figures*

The Federal Trade Commission reports that Elon Musk Impersonators have made more than $2 million in recent years as a part of various cryptocurrency scams. The nature of this scam is in the form of a "giveaway". You will find tweets from famous personalities like Elon Musk, Barack Obama, or Joe Biden which will mention something about a giveaway.

THE MESSAGE WILL STATE that if you send cryptocurrencies to the given wallet, they will be multiplied immediately and returned to you. People who have sent the currencies have done so to the wallet of a fraudster. There is no giveaway or any scheme; impersonators create fake profiles for these authority figures and try to trick people into sending them cryptocurrency. Once they receive the currencies, they sell them on any exchange to earn a profit.

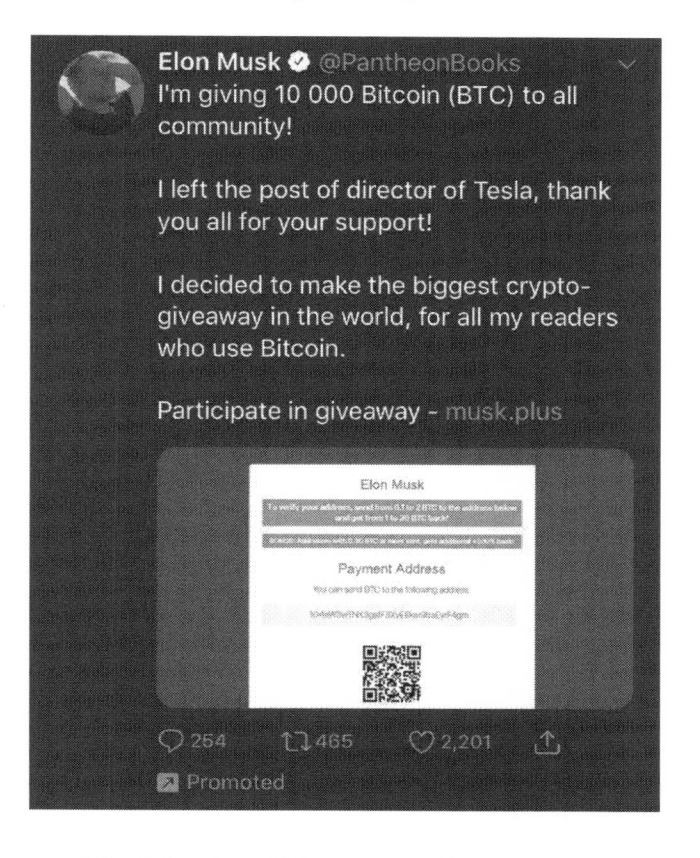

**Figure 11:** A fake "Elon Musk" Twitter profile running a crypto scam. Note the Twitter handle not matching the name

### Use of Pop Culture

Using pop culture to trick people has become increasingly common in the cryptocurrency market. This creates a golden opportunity for scammers who hype a pop culture-based currency to raise money from passionate investors. After they have earned enough money, they simply vanish and there won't be any existence of the coin or the people who were initially promoting it. Mando was one such cryptocurrency that was created around Disney-themed show *The Mandalorian*. Even after losing thousands of dollars, people did not learn and they again got scammed through the *Squid Game* cryptocurrency. We will discuss this one in detail in a later section of this chapter.

## Types of Crypto Scams

In the previous section, we talked about what happens in the common cryptocurrency scams. Now let's get into a bit more detail and discuss the various types of scams that have taken place. Broadly, there are two categories of crypto scams:

- Trying to gain access to your crypto wallet. This would include getting information that gives out details about your private key and is a form of hacking into your account. Note: No cryptocurrency exchange will ever ask for your private key. So be sure to watch out for phishing emails from scammers attempting to impersonate Coinbase or Binance.
- Transferring crypto directly to the fraudster's account by impersonating someone or using fraudulent business opportunities.

Under these two broad categories, crypto scams take various other forms which we have discussed as follows:

### Social Engineering Scams

These scams use manipulation and psychologically pressure the victims to gain information related to their crypto wallets. The victims are made to believe they are dealing with a trusted person like a government agency, community member, colleague, or a reputed business. The whole process is to mess with their minds so that they do not hesitate to share information or even send cryptocurrency directly to the scammer. The various scams under this segment are:

- Romance Scams: Fraudsters use dating apps to make victims feel they are in a romantic relationship after which they ask for money from them. Cryptocurrency transactions make up a huge part of these scams.
- Imposter and Giveaway Scams.
- Phishing Scams: They are a way to obtain information related to cryptocurrency wallets and private keys. The process is that the victims receive emails that direct them to a specially curated website that tries to capture the above-mentioned information.
- Blackmail Scams: Here the victim is blackmailed into providing information about private keys or transferring cryptocurrencies to the scammer's wallet. They might also be given threats about unpleasant consequences if they failed to comply.

### BUSINESS OPPORTUNITY SCAMS

Always remember the phrase that if something is too good to be true, then it probably is. There is no such thing as "get rich quick" or "make millions overnight" in the crypto market. People who have made millions did so as a result of speculation. Most of them had no idea or control over the fact that cryptocurrencies would make them rich. That is why if you hear somebody claiming that they would make you rich or provide guaranteed returns in the crypto market, run in the opposite direction because it is a scam.

### PUMP AND DUMP Scams

Pump and dump scams are nothing new. They've plagued the stock market for years as scammers have artificially inflated the prices of penny stocks before cashing out. This is a phenomenon where fraudsters first pump the price of a cryptocurrency by spreading false information about the currency and its prospects. (Recall the example of DeTrade in Chapter 4.). Then, after the price of the coin has been boosted, the fraudsters sell all their holdings to make a huge profit and leave the other investors at a loss for words and money.

THESE ARE NOW BECOMING INCREASINGLY common on social media with invitations to "insider trading" groups appearing in people's direct messages on Facebook, Instagram and Twitter. Some of these now blatantly advertise themselves as "pump groups".

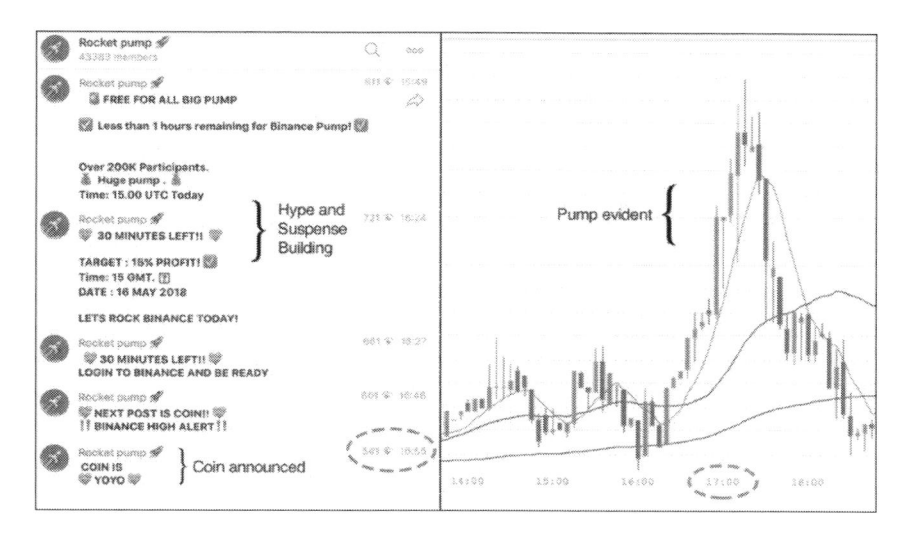

**Figure 12:** An example of a Pump and Dump group on Telegram and subsequent market activity on the targeted coin (Source: ResearchGate)

THESE SCAMS ARE ALSO INCREASINGLY prevalent in the comment sections of cryptocurrency YouTube channels. Remember if anyone approaches you on social media offering a get-rich-quick trading opportunity, avoid it like the plague. A good rule of thumb is to remember that anyone promising that they know which crypto coin will pump next, likely has an ulterior motive.

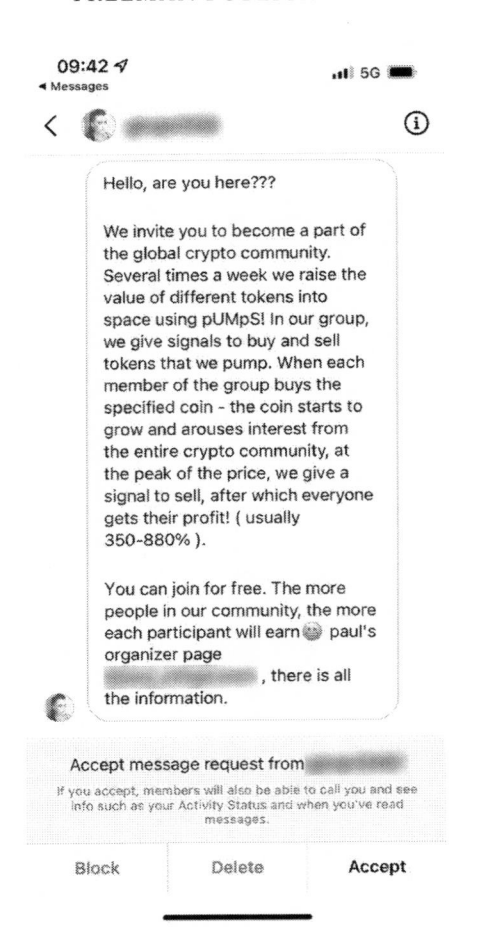

**Figure 13:** An example of a Pump and Dump group recruiting message, sent via Instagram

FAKE TRADING SCAMS

Ever been approached by a "Bitcoin trader" on social media?

UNFORTUNATELY THIS HAPPENED to one of our readers, who we'll just call D. D allowed me to share her story in full in order to prevent others suffering the same fate, so I've decided to re-print it here.

This was originally published in our daily newsletter on December 3$^{rd}$ 2021, to sign up to our newsletter just go to

HTTPS://FREEMANPUBLICATIONS.COM/BONUS

---

A READER, who I'll just call D, emailed me yesterday to ask if I had heard of a certain brokerage website.

I hadn't... which automatically raises a red flag seeing as I do this for a living.

The website in question appears to be somewhat legit at first glance, claiming to be registered in Switzerland. So I asked D why she was inquiring about the website. D shared her story and has graciously allowed me to reprint it to help other readers avoid the same fate.

*"I WAS USING [scam website] as training to learn investing. I made an investment of $250.00 US and a broker worked with me and showed me trades and of course as we traded the money initially invested grew.*

*WE DID a little investing with crypto through their platform. I signed up for CoinBase and bought Bitcoin that we transferred over. Altogether my*

*investment was $4,750 Canadian. I attempted to withdraw money from the [scam website] account to my CoinSmart account and I received an email saying that in order to get my funds I had to pay a liquidation fee of $4,900 CDN. I didn't have the $4,900 on the spot. Our e-transfers are limited which in hindsight is a good thing.*

*IT DIDN'T SEEM RIGHT, why did I have to pay a fee to withdraw funds? I spoke with CoinSmart and they told me that the email I received about the liquidation fee didn't come from them."*

I ADVISED D to not pay any kind of "liquidation fee" and to cut her losses at this point. The "broker" is still contacting her - which is part of the scam.

HERE'S a breakdown of exactly how the scam works

1. A broker contacts you, usually via social media, asking you sign up and deposit a small amount of money with them.

2. These companies will access your computer via some kind of remote desktop software like AnyDesk and conduct "trades" on your account (while explaining what they're doing to make it seem legit). These trades will always be profitable because they aren't real and instead use dummy software to replicate real trades.

3. The company gets you to wire a larger amount of money to them (this can be in fiat currency, but more commonly now using crypto).

.   .   .

4. More fake trades occur with the intention of getting you to wire them even more money.

5. If you ever try to withdraw the money... either the company ghosts you on the spot... or they will start some BS about "withdrawal fees" or "liquidation fees" which are often more than your entire investment.

---

Now here's how to avoid how this ever happening to you

1. Only use well known brokerages (like CoinBase, Binance or Crypto.com). If you aren't sure about a brokerage, look them up in their local jurisdiction. All brokers (stocks, crypto, FOREX) are required to register with their local financial authority (like FINRA in the US or the FCA in the United Kingdom) and will have a unique license number which you can look up online. For example, Coinbase has been licensed by FINRA and the SEC since 2010.

You can lookup US brokers at
https://brokercheck.finra.org/

And in the UK you can go to
https://register.fca.org.uk/

. . .

2. Never allow anyone to trade on your behalf - either via wiring money to them or by allowing them to access your computer via a remote desktop.

3. If it smells like a scam, it probably is.

## CLOUD MINING SCAMS

CLOUD MINING SCAMS have been around since cryptocurrency first really started becoming popular in 2016. The premise is similar to any Ponzi scheme. Websites will ask you to deposit either fiat money or cryptocurrency to be part of a cryptocurrency mining group. Usually they will promise huge gains of up to 1.5% PER DAY.

MANY OF THESE websites with display fake figures in an attempt to provide their legitimacy. These include listed giant number of users or statistics claiming they have been in business for many years. Other tell-tale signs of a scam are attempts to keep all communication on Telegram or WhatsApp as opposed to channels like email.

 **36.9M**
REGISTERED USERS

 **174**
COUNTRIES SUPPORTED

**Figure 14:** USDminer claims to have 36 million registered users, however the website was less than 1 month old at the time of writing

THE FOLLOWING active websites are confirmed to be scam mining operations

- Xminer
- Miner Plus
- Pageminer
- Nhash
- USDminer
- Muxminer

*FAKE BITCOIN LENDING **Schemes***

Another common crypto scam is in the form of a "lending scheme", where you receive regular payouts for the cryptocurrencies that you have supposedly lent to the borrower. We should note that there are legitimate cryptocurrency lending schemes via platforms like Celsius, Block-Fi or Crypto.com.

However there are also many outright scam platforms, some of which made off with tens of millions in investor money. Here are the 2 most prominent ones.

*BITCONNECT*

This is one of the most famous crypto scams, and became so big that it even made the top 10 list of coins according to market cap. They offered a kind of lending scheme where your currencies would be locked and you would receive a payout regularly. Their project initially claimed they had an AI-enabled trading bot that guaranteed abnormal profits for all their holders. The impossibly high payouts (1% daily compounding interest) combined with the multi-level marketing nature of the platform meant that the initial payouts were only funded by new money being deposited into the scheme, and not by the trading bot itself.

·  ·  ·

*Davorcoin*

Similar to Bitconnect, Davorcoin was introduced as an ICO and had lending programs where the investors could receive a payout. There was a presence of a pyramid-like affiliate program and fake promises of a crypto debit card which never saw the light of day.

## Case Study: Squid Game Crypto Scam

On September 17, 2021, a Korean show called *Squid Game* was released on Netflix. The plotline centered around hundreds of cash-strapped people fighting simple games in a do-or-die situation to win a huge cash prize. The show became an instant hit across the world and reached the #1 position within a matter of days. Consequently, the Internet started flooding with *Squid Game* memes and posts. When the whole world was obsessed with the show in October 2021, a group of developers released a Squid Game token (SQUID) which was listed on CoinMarketCap.

THE COIN WAS THEMED SURROUNDING the popular show and started trading at $0.02 per token on October 26th. By November, the price of the token had risen to $2,800, which meant an increase of 14,300,000% in a matter of weeks. The phenomenal increase had something fishy about it. You guessed it right, it was a classic example of a pump-and-dump scheme, but the public was yet to understand that.

Now let's deconstruct what happened and how the price rose by such high margins. A group of developers who have conveniently stayed anonymous launched this crypto project called Squid Game. This token would be used as an entry pass or "buy-in" to Squid Game-themed games like Red Light/Green Light and Honeycomb. The winners of these games would be rewarded with cash prizes. When they won a game, they would be rewarded with "marbles", another reference from the show. The developers used an anti-dumping strategy, which implied that unless a player won a marble, they wouldn't be able to sell their tokens. All of it sounds perfectly fine in theory until we come to the real catch of the situation. The developers had yet to come up with a real game for this Squid Game project. This meant that the players had no option to win the marbles because there was no game for them to play. Until they won the marbles, there was no way to sell the tokens, which means they were trapped in a situation over which they had no control and there was nothing to be done. The players thought they were waiting for the games to begin, but that never happened. The craze surrounding the show skyrocketed the prices of the token, and eventually, the developers cashed out the coins and took away $12 million. This is nothing but an outright fraud and the developers should immediately be put behind bars.

MORE THAN ANYTHING, this is a lesson for all crypto investors to not gamble on crypto created around the latest hype. The hype will die down soon, and so will the price of the token. The phenomenal rise is simply a trick to keep you interested and invested. Just like there are penny stock frauds in the stock markets, there are bogus tokens and rug pulls in the crypto market. Would you avoid the stock market because of those penny stocks? If not, then why should you avoid the crypto space because of these scams? The key to succeeding in any market is the same—go for the genuine stocks and tokens. Pick the best cryptos, not something random like Squid Game.

# 11 CRYPTO PREDICTIONS FOR 2022

Every year in our daily newsletter (which you can join at https://freemanpublications.com/bonus) I like to make predictions for the coming financial year.

This year I thought I'd do something a little more permanent and print them in our book. So here we go, my 11 crypto predictions for 2022.

1. A Q1 bear market will see Bitcoin drop below $40,000 before reaching $100,000 by the end of the year.
2. Another Bitcoin ETF will launch, except this one will track the spot price of Bitcoin rather than Bitcoin futures like BITO.
3. Ethereum will become the next Trillion Dollar coin (this would put the price of 1 ETH at around $7,300).
4. But they still won't move to Proof of Stake until 2023.
5. Solana will reach a market cap of over $200 Billion by the end of the year.
6. Solana will also "decouple" from Bitcoin, meaning that its price will move independent of Bitcoin prices.

7. At least 1 major country will announce that some of its national debt has been collateralized using stablecoins.
8. A new government body will be created to regulate cryptoassets (and this will be a good thing in the long run).
9. A least 1 Fortune 500 company will allow full-time employees to be paid in cryptocurrency.
10. There will be at least 1 major fraud case in the NFT market.
11. NFT marketplace OpenSea will do traditional IPO, despite calls for the company to do an ICO on the crypto markets instead.
12. Blockchain gaming will provide a new onboarding into the crypto space, which will significantly increase the overall number of people owning cryptocurrency.
13. At least one meme coin with a $1 Billion market cap will completely collapse.

Feel free to email me your own predictions at admin@freemanpublications.com.

# CONCLUSION: AMARA'S LAW AND PLAYING THE LONG GAME

Roy Amara isn't exactly a household name, except in Futurism circles. The Stanford researcher who passed away in 2007, gave us one of the most poignant quotes about technology in the past 100 years, which has since been coined "Amara's Law"

*"We tend to overestimate the effect of a technology in the short run and underestimate the effect in the long run".*

This is no more true than in the crypto world. Whenever you come across articles about cryptocurrencies, you will find two extremes being portrayed - either the article claims that cryptos are the ultimate savior of humankind or they will caution you because they are purely speculative and always bring you eternal doom.

The truth is that while cryptocurrency is new, within just a few years of their existence, it has managed to make its mark on us and the economy. Like it or not, cryptocurrency is here to stay.

However, you must understand that this is not a linear journey to riches. There is going to be continued volatility in this space for the next 5 years at least. And you should fully expect any cryptocurrency you buy to decline by at least 50% at some point if you are planning to hold it for at least five years.

But if you can stomach those downturns, many of these millionaire maker assets will be the ones that allow you to retire early, put your kids through college, and create generational wealth for you and your loved ones. To illustrate this, let's take one final look at Bitcoin price fluctuations.

## The Rollercoaster of Bitcoin Prices

Since its inception, Bitcoin has been notorious for having the highest highs and coming down to the lowest lows within months. Bitcoin first hit $1 in April 2011. In July 2011, the value rose to $29.60, which means a 2,960% increase within three months. After a sharp recession, the value came down to $2.05 by November. After an uneventful 2012, Bitcoin rose rapidly in 2013 from $13.28 in the beginning to $230 in April and then fell drastically to $68.50 within a few weeks. The year ended with an all-time high of $1,237.55, only to fall by almost 44% within the next three days. Bitcoin struggled with its prices throughout 2014 and 2015 with no major highs or lows. By the end of 2016, Bitcoin was priced at $900 and increased by 122% in the next six months.

However, the real high came in December 2017 when Bitcoin skyrocketed to $19,345.49. This was the moment when it truly attracted the attention of the entire world and all spheres of the economy. The next two years were again uneventful, and prices fell to around $6,000 by December 2019. When the economy was shut down due to the COVID-19 Pandemic, Bitcoin prices again showed bursts of activity after starting 2020 at $6,965.72. The year ended for Bitcoin on the highest-ever note after increasing 416% from the beginning of the year and reaching $29,000 in December 2020. Bitcoin had reached a bull run and kept smashing its records by reaching $40,000 in January 2021 and $63,000 in April 2021. Prices started falling soon after, and the summer of 2021 saw a 50% decline.

However, Bitcoin again reached an all-time high of $67,549.14 in November 2021, only to fall by 22% within a month when the economy started having a scare about the Omicron variant of COVID-19.

Since 2009, here are some of the volatility events Bitcoin has undergone:

- 10 drawdowns of over 30%
- 5 drawdowns of over 50%
- 3 drawdowns of over 80%
- 1 drawdown of over 90%

The most important thing to take from this though, is that even with all these pullbacks, Bitcoin and the entire cryptocurrency space continues to move into new highs. In 2021 alone we saw the value of the cryptocurrency industry go from $800 Billion to over $2.8 Trillion in just 10 months.

## Play Smart

As you can already see, drawdowns are an integral part of investing in crypto and you should not go for investing in this market if that bothers you. Our suggestion is to dedicate 5-10% of your portfolio to cryptocurrency. In this way, even if you lose everything, your maximum loss will be limited to only 10%.

If the bullish thesis is correct, then that 5% can be worth 50% of your portfolio or more. This asymmetric bet will ensure a high upside and minimal downside. Although in the short term most crypto prices still mirror Bitcoin prices, you can end up enjoying a greater gain percentage if you hold different types of currencies. For instance, when prices of both Bitcoin and Ethereum are rising, the rate of increase in Ethereum might be greater than that of Bitcoin. Even if the total value of your portfolio is huge, start small with crypto. The amount invested should be something that you are comfortable losing.

No matter what everyone says, there is no rule that you have to invest in crypto to make money. Some people simply don't have the required risk appetite. However, there is no doubt that crypto is the next big financial asset class, and the riskiest financial move you can make over the next decade is <u>not owning any.</u>

As we have explained through the course of this book, investing in crypto does not have to be very difficult. Whenever you feel like you are having doubts, just refer to this book.

Alternatively, you can email us at

<u>admin@freemanpublications.com</u> if you would like something clarified. We answer every single reader email.

2021 was a chaotic year, so as we move into 2022, we wish you the best of luck with your investing!

One final word from us. If this book has helped you in any way, we'd appreciate it if you left a review on Amazon.

Reviews are the lifeblood of our business. We read every single one and incorporate your feedback into our future book projects.

To leave an Amazon review, go to
https://freemanpublications.com/leaveareview

# OTHER BOOKS BY FREEMAN PUBLICATIONS (AVAILABLE ON AMAZON & AUDIBLE)

You can learn more about our other titles by going to

https://freemanpublications.com/books

Or if you prefer listening you can find our Audiobooks at

https://freemanpublications.com/audiobooks

# ACKNOWLEDGMENTS

This book is a team effort, and while I get to be the face of the business and receive all the kind messages from readers, I can't ignore the people who helped make this book what it was.

Thank you first to our content team for their writing, editing, and proofreading efforts and dealing with my persistent questions about why specific changes needed to be made.

Thank you to Mark Greenberg, our superstar narrator, who has really become "the voice" of Freeman Publications over the past year.

Thank you to Ed Fahy over at UBF for always being there every time I needed to make a minor update to the book interior.

Thank you to the 400+ Freeman readers who participated in our advanced reader program for this book. Your notes and feedback were invaluable in going from the final draft to the finished product.

A special mention must go to Carlota Wilhite and Vinay Narayanan for their incredibly detailed feedback ranging from things we didn't clarify well enough to points we outright missed. Without your input, this book simply would not have been as good as it is today.

Thank you to our hundreds of readers on social media for your words of encouragement throughout this project.

Finally, thank you to my family, whose initial uncertainty of "are you still doing that book thing" has blossomed into full support for my vision here at Freeman Publications. This means more than you will ever know.

Oliver

London, England

January, 2022

# REFERENCES

*A timeline of the history of cryptocurrency.* (2021, August 31). Tech Guide. https://www.techguide.-com.au/news/cryptocurrency/a-timeline-of-the-history-of-cryptocurrency/

abhijithoyur. (2021, September 10). *Different ways to convert Bitcoin to fiat currency.* Geeksfor-Geeks. https://www.geeksforgeeks.org/different-ways-to-convert-bitcoin-to-fiat-currency/

Agarwal, K. (2019). *Are there taxes on Bitcoins?* Investopedia. https://www.investopedia.com/articles/investing/040515/are-there-taxes-bitcoins.asp

Amundi. (2021, November 2). *Can stablecoins bring major disruption to the financial system?* Amundi Research Center. https://research-center.amundi.com/article/can-stablecoins-bring-major-disruption-financial-system

Analyst, Z. (2021, November 18). *Silvergate Capital: Riding the crypto wave (NYSE:SI) | Seeking Alpha.* Seekingalpha.com. https://seekingalpha.com/article/4470669-silvergate-capital-riding-the-crypto-wave

BBVA. (2017, November 10). *A basic dictionary of blockchain: 10 terms you should know | BBVA.* NEWS BBVA. https://www.bbva.com/en/basic-dictionary-blockchain-10-terms-know/

Beginners, B. for. (2019, April 15). *Case Study: Top 5 scams in the history of crypto.* Medium. https://medium.com/@bitcoinforbeginners/case-study-top-5-scams-in-the-history-of-crypto-df8a01443bc6

Berkowitz, B. (2021, May 16). *Is Theta token the next Ethereum or the next Dogecoin?* Www.nas-daq.com. https://www.nasdaq.com/articles/is-theta-token-the-next-ethereum-or-the-next-dogecoin-2021-05-16

# References

Bhasin, K. (2021, October 28). *Matt Damon is the Face of Crypto.com.* Www.bloomberg.com. https://www.bloomberg.com/news/articles/2021-10-28/matt-damon-to-promote-crypto-com-in-race-to-attract-new-users

Blanchet, B. (2021, May 18). *Elon Musk impersonators have made over $2 million in crypto scams.* Complex. https://www.complex.com/pop-culture/people-pretending-to-be-elon-musk-crypto-scams

Blockgenicon, B. (2018, November 23). *Asymmetric cryptography in Blockchains | Hacker Noon.* Hackernoon.com. https://hackernoon.com/asymmetric-cryptography-in-blockchains-d1a4c1654a7

*BLOK—Amplify Transformational Data Sharing ETF—Amplify ETFs.* (n.d.). Amplifyetfs.com. https://amplifyetfs.com/blok.html

Catalini, C., & Massari, J. (2021, August 10). *Stablecoins and the future of money.* Harvard Business Review. https://hbr.org/2021/08/stablecoins-and-the-future-of-money

Chang, H. (2020, March 25). *Understanding the value of Non-Fungible Tokens (NFT).* Medium. https://medium.com/@changhugo/understanding-the-value-of-non-fungible-tokens-nft-49d2713bdfc4

Clark, K. (2021a). *Briefing: Stripe adds crypto investor Matt Huang to board.* The Information. https://www.theinformation.com/briefings/d5b6ee

Clark, K. (2021b, October 19). *Multicoin capital targets $250 million for third Crypto VC fund.* The Information. https://www.theinformation.com/articles/multicoin-capital-targets-250-million-for-third-crypto-vc-fund

Clark, K., & Miller, H. (2021, October 4). *Andreessen Horowitz values developer of NFT game Axie Infinity at $3 Billion.* The Information. https://www.theinformation.com/articles/andreessen-horowitz-values-developer-of-nft-game-axie-infinity-at-3-billion

Cohen, E. (2021, July 1). *A cryptocurrency timeline: From eCash to Ethereum.* Vincent. https://www.withvincent.com/learn/cryptocurrency-timeline

Coinbase. (2021a, September 8). *The SEC has told us it wants to sue us over Lend. We don't know why.* Medium. https://blog.coinbase.com/the-sec-has-told-us-it-wants-to-sue-us-over-lend-we-have-no-idea-why-a3a1b6507009

Coinbase. (2021b, October 12). *Coinbase NFT is coming soon: join the waitlist today for early access.* Medium. https://blog.coinbase.com/coinbase-nft-is-coming-soon-join-the-waitlist-today-for-early-access-cc7bac29fd72

*Coinbase strategy teardown: How Coinbase grew into the King Midas of crypto doing $1B in revenue.* (2021, October 19). CB Insights Research. https://www.cbinsights.com/research/report/coinbase-strategy-teardown/#kingmaker

Conti, R. (2021, April 29). *What you need to know about Non-Fungible Tokens (NFTs).* Forbes Advisor. https://www.forbes.com/advisor/investing/nft-non-fungible-token/

Conway, L. (2021, November 4). *Blockchain, explained.* Investopedia. https://www.investopedia.-com/terms/b/blockchain.asp

Copeland, T. (2021, March 11). *Beeple NFT artwork sells for $69.3 million in Christie's auction.* Decrypt. https://decrypt.co/60971/beeples-nft-artwork-sells-for-60-3-million-in-christies-auction

Dale. (2018, February 6). *Is Falcon Coin a scam or Ponzi Scheme? Full Review exposes It!* Living More Working Less. https://www.livingmoreworkingless.com/falcon-coin-scam/

Danial, K. (n.d.). *What is Cryptocurrency?* Dummies. https://www.dummies.com/personal-finance/what-is-cryptocurrency/

De Bode, I., Higginson, M., & Niederkorn, M. (n.d.). *Central bank digital currency and stablecoin: Early coexistence on an uncertain road | McKinsey.* Www.mckinsey.com. https://www.mckinsey.-com/industries/financial-services/our-insights/cbdc-and-stablecoins-early-coexistence-on-an-uncertain-road

Deloitte. (n.d.). *The business benefit of using cryptocurrency.* Deloitte United States. https://www2.deloitte.com/us/en/pages/audit/articles/corporates-using-crypto.html

Dixon, C. (2021, October 7). *Why Web3 matters.* Future. https://future.a16z.com/why-web3-matters/

Edwards, J. (2019). *Bitcoin's price history.* Investopedia. https://www.investopedia.com/articles/forex/121815/bitcoins-price-history.asp

Elena. (2020, November 27). *What you need to know about Stellar, the altcoin that's out of this world.* The Capital. https://medium.com/the-capital/what-you-need-to-know-about-stellar-the-altcoin-thats-out-of-this-world-eb165c92f051

Elliott, V. (2021, September 30). *Some Axie Infinity players amassed fortunes — now the Philippine government wants its cut.* Rest of World. https://restofworld.org/2021/axie-players-are-facing-taxes/

Fintelics. (2021, June 9). *How to make money with NFTs—Fintelics—Medium.* Medium; Medium. https://fintelics.medium.com/how-to-make-money-with-nfts-15a1e4718d15#:~:text=You%20can%20stake%20your%20NFTs

Frank, J., & Silverstein, S. (2019, February 13). *Vitalik Buterin created one of the world's largest cryptocurrencies in his early twenties—here's how he did it and why.* Business Insider. https://www.businessinsider.in/vitalik-buterin-created-one-of-the-worlds-largest-cryptocurrencies-in-his-early-twenties-heres-how-he-did-it-and-why/articleshow/67978060.cms

Frankenfield, J. (2019a). *Consensus Mechanism (Cryptocurrency).* Investopedia. https://www.investopedia.com/terms/c/consensus-mechanism-cryptocurrency.asp

Frankenfield, J. (2019b, May 5). *Cryptocurrency.* Investopedia. https://www.investopedia.-com/terms/c/cryptocurrency.asp

Frankenfield, J. (2021a, April 26). *Altcoin.* Investopedia. https://www.investopedia.com/terms/a/altcoin.asp

Frankenfield, J. (2021b, June 4). *Ethereum.* Investopedia. https://www.investopedia.com/terms/e/ethereum.asp

*Global X Blockchain ETF (BKCH).* (n.d.). Global X ETFs. https://www.globalxetfs.com/funds/bkch/

Greifeld, K. (2021, October 21). *ProShares Bitcoin ETF tops $1 Billion assets in just 2 days.* Www.bloomberg.com. https://www.bloomberg.com/news/articles/2021-10-20/proshares-bitcoin-etf-tops-1-billion-in-assets-in-just-two-days

Hayes, A. (2021, August 26). *Is Ethereum more important than Bitcoin?* Investopedia. https://www.investopedia.com/articles/investing/032216/ethereum-more-important-bitcoin.asp

Hertig, A. (2021, July 22). *How do Ethereum smart contracts work?* Www.coindesk.com. https://www.coindesk.com/learn/how-do-ethereum-smart-contracts-work/

Hung, J. (2021, July 29). *Are NFTs just a fad Or here to stay?* Www.linkedin.com. https://www.linkedin.com/pulse/nfts-just-fad-here-stay-jonathan-hung

Iger, B. (2021, June 4). *Cryptocurrency explained: How does Cryptocurrency work?* Masterclass.com. https://www.masterclass.com/articles/cryptocurrency-explained#how-does-cryptocurrency-work

Jain, P. (2020). *TechDay—Impact of blockchain technology on financial services.* Techdayhq.com. https://techdayhq.com/community/articles/impact-of-block-chain-technology-on-financial-services

Jegede, D. O. (2021, November 23). *10 altcoins to look out for in 2022.* Trend Online. https://www.trend-online.com/cryptocurrency/altcoins-2022/

Jones, B. (2018, October 5). *The cryptocurrency timeline.* ICS-Digital. https://www.ics-digital.com/the-cryptocurrency-timeline/

Kameir, C. (2020, February 18). *Council Post: Blockchain investment opportunity: Fiat money.* Forbes. https://www.forbes.com/sites/forbesfinancecouncil/2020/02/18/blockchain-investment-opportunity-fiat-money/?sh=341f59bd277d

Kharpal, A. (2021, April 6). *Cryptocurrency market value tops $2 trillion for the first time as ethereum hits record high.* CNBC. https://www.cnbc.com/2021/04/06/cryptocurrency-market-cap-tops-2-trillion-for-the-first-time.html

Lexology. (2021, November 2). *Stablecoins: Latest disruption to traditional banking.* Lexology. https://www.lexology.com/pro/insideview/stablecoins-latest-disruption-to-traditional-banking

Leyes, K. (2021, December). *3 ways to make money with Non-Fungible Tokens (NFTs).* Entrepreneur. https://www.entrepreneur.com/article/368122

Liebkind, J. (2021, October 30). *Beware of these five Bitcoin scams.* Investopedia. https://www.investopedia.com/articles/forex/042315/beware-these-five-bitcoin-scams.asp

Livni, E., & Lipton, E. (2021, September 5). Crypto banking and decentralized finance, explained. *The New York Times*. https://www.nytimes.com/2021/09/05/us/politics/cryptocurrency-explainer.html#:~:text=What%20is%20DeFi%3F

Locke, T. (2021, January 9). *Thinking of buying bitcoin? What experts say about big crypto concerns: "You have to be mentally prepared."* CNBC. https://www.cnbc.com/2021/01/09/what-experts-say-about-cryptocurrency-bitcoin-concerns.html

Maring, J. (2021, April 1). *How TikTok influencer & others lost money in "Mando" cryptocurrency scam*. ScreenRant. https://screenrant.com/tiktok-mandalorian-cryptocurrency-scam-explained/

McWhinney, J. (2019). *Can Bitcoin kill central banks?* Investopedia. https://www.investopedia.com/articles/investing/050715/can-bitcoin-kill-central-banks.asp

Michael. (2020, November 27). *Plus Token (PLUS) scam—Anatomy of a Ponzi*. Boxmining. https://boxmining.com/plus-token-ponzi/

Miller, H. (2021, November 4). *New York takes on Miami; Square's Bitcoin revenue stumbles*. The Information. https://www.theinformation.com/articles/new-york-takes-on-miami-square-s-bitcoin-revenue-stumbles

MintDice. (2019, September 26). *The psychology of cheap coins and why it's worth studying*. The Capital. https://medium.com/the-capital/the-psychology-of-cheap-coins-and-why-its-worth-studying-14e1d1a2b3d8

Napoletano, E. (2021, June 30). *Bitcoin IRA: How to invest for retirement with cryptocurrency*. Forbes Advisor. https://www.forbes.com/advisor/retirement/bitcoin-ira/

Newton, C. (2021, October 13). *How Axie Infinity is turning gaming on its head*. The Verge. https://www.theverge.com/2021/10/13/22725083/axie-infinity-sky-mavis-blockchain-economy-game-pokemon

Novak, M. (2021, November 1). *Squid Game cryptocurrency scammers make off with $2.1 million*. Gizmodo. https://gizmodo.com/squid-game-cryptocurrency-scammers-make-off-with-2-1-m-1847972824

Ohanian, A. (2021, September 15). *Vitalik Buterin: The 100 most influential people of 2021*. Time. https://time.com/collection/100-most-influential-people-2021/6095980/vitalik-buterin/

Parashar, R. (2021, September 21). *What is Uniswap, and why is it useful?* NDTV Gadgets 360. https://gadgets.ndtv.com/cryptocurrency/features/what-is-uniswap-cryptocurrency-why-is-it-useful-2547964

Prasad, E. (2021, May 24). *Five myths about cryptocurrency*. Brookings. https://www.brookings.edu/opinions/five-myths-about-cryptocurrency/

Reiff, N. (2020, January 21). *What Is the Grayscale Bitcoin Trust?* Investopedia. https://www.investopedia.com/news/why-buy-expensive-bitcoin-etf-instead-actual-bitcoin/

Reiff, N. (2021a, August 26). *Were there Cryptocurrencies before Bitcoin?* Investopedia. https://www.investopedia.com/tech/were-there-cryptocurrencies-bitcoin/

Reiff, N. (2021b, November 7). *Blockchain ETF.* Investopedia. https://www.investopedia.com/tech/how-blockchain-etfs-work/

Rodeck, D. (2021a, March 26). *What is Ethereum and how does it work?* Forbes Advisor. https://www.forbes.com/advisor/investing/what-is-ethereum-ether/

Rodeck, D. (2021b, November 16). *Cryptocurrency taxes 2021: What you need to know.* Forbes Advisor. https://www.forbes.com/advisor/investing/cryptocurrency-taxes/

Royal, J., & Voigt, K. (2021, December 3). *What Is Cryptocurrency? Beginners guide to digital cash.* NerdWallet. https://www.nerdwallet.com/article/investing/cryptocurrency-7-things-to-know

Schreier, J. (2021, November 13). *Blockchain in gaming is all the rage for no good reason.* Www.bloomberg.com. https://www.bloomberg.com/news/newsletters/2021-11-12/crypto-in-video-games-is-all-the-rage-but-why

Sergeenkov, A. (2021, December 11). *5 ways to earn passive income from NFTs.* Www.coindesk.com. https://www.coindesk.com/learn/5-ways-to-earn-passive-income-from-nfts/

Seth, S. (2021). *Central Bank Digital Currency (CBDC).* Investopedia. https://www.investopedia.com/terms/c/central-bank-digital-currency-cbdc.asp

Shaw, R. (n.d.). *Blockchain key terms, explained.* KDnuggets. https://www.kdnuggets.com/2017/11/blockchain-key-terms-explained.html

Shetty, N. (2021, May 19). *5 ways to smartly invest in Bitcoin.* Finextra Research. https://www.finextra.com/blogposting/20333/5-ways-to-smartly-invest-in-bitcoin

Sigalos, M. (2021, August 10). *Coinbase profits surge following volatile stretch of cryptocurrency trading.* CNBC. https://www.cnbc.com/2021/08/10/coinbase-coin-earnings-q2-2021.html

*Silvergate expands reach of Bitcoin collateralized U.S. Dollar loans, announces Fidelity Digital Assets as Custody Provider.* (2021, March 29). Www.businesswire.com. https://www.businesswire.com/news/home/20210329005050/en/Silvergate-Expands-Reach-of-Bitcoin-Collateralized-U.S.-Dollar-Loans-Announces-Fidelity-Digital-Assets-as-Custody-Provider

Staff, B. (2021, July 28). *Cryptocurrencies can never replace fiat money.* Blockonomist. https://medium.com/blockonomist/cryptocurrencies-can-never-replace-fiat-money-52a0291b23da

Stokel-Walker, C. (2021, November 2). *How a Squid Game crypto scam got away with millions.* Wired. https://www.wired.com/story/squid-game-coin-crypto-scam/

Sukhadeve, A. (2021, November 20). *Top 10 Altcoins that are set to explode In 2022.* Analyticsinsight.net. https://www.analyticsinsight.net/top-10-altcoins-that-are-set-to-explode-in-2022/

Telegraph.co.uk. (2018, May 25). *Cryptocurrencies: a timeline.* The Telegraph. https://www.telegraph.co.uk/technology/digital-money/the-history-of-cryptocurrency/

Tepper, T. (2021, February 26). Coinbase IPO: Here's what you need to know. *Forbes.* https://www.forbes.com/advisor/investing/coinbase-ipo-direct-listing/

The Investopedia Team. (2021, November 15). *Terra.* Investopedia. https://www.investopedia.com/terra-5209502

*The ultimate guide to chainlink | What is LINK coin?* (n.d.). Cryptonews.com. https://cryptonews.com/coins/chainlink/

Trails, B. (n.d.). *Digital signatures in Blockchains: The present and future.* Bison Trails. https://bisontrails.co/digital-signatures/

Van Boom, D. (2021, April 13). *Forget Bitcoin: Inside the insane world of altcoin cryptocurrency trading.* CNET. https://www.cnet.com/features/beyond-bitcoin-the-wild-world-of-altcoin-cryptocurrency-trading/

Ventures, F. (2020, January 6). *What is Web 3.0 & why it matters.* Medium. https://medium.com/fabric-ventures/what-is-web-3-0-why-it-matters-934eb07f3d2b

Vermaak, W. (2021, December 7). *What is Web 3.0? | CoinMarketCap.* Coinmarketcap.com. https://coinmarketcap.com/alexandria/article/what-is-web-3-0

Voigt, K., & Rosen, A. (2021, November 4). *What is Blockchain? The technology behind Cryptocurrency, explained.* NerdWallet. https://www.nerdwallet.com/article/investing/blockchain

Wangman, R. (2021, November 2). *Crypto-backed loans don't require a credit check, but your collateral isn't immune to market swings.* Business Insider. https://www.businessinsider.com/personal-finance/what-is-crypto-lending?IR=T

Wathen, J. (2018, January 19). *Amplify Transformational Data Sharing ETF: 3 things to know about this Blockchain ETF.* The Motley Fool. https://www.fool.com/investing/2018/01/19/amplify-transformational-data-sharing-etf-3-things.aspx

*What is Bitcoin?* (n.d.). PCMAG. https://www.pcmag.com/encyclopedia/term/bitcoin

*What is Hedera Hashgraph? (HBAR) | Kraken.* (n.d.). Www.kraken.com. https://www.kraken.com/en-us/learn/what-is-hedera-hashgraph-hbar

*Why Solana is the top-performing cryptocurrency of 2021.* (2021, September 7). The Mail & Guardian. https://mg.co.za/special-reports/2021-09-07-why-solana-is-the-top-performing-cryptocurrency-of-2021/#:~:text=What%20makes%20Solana%20unique%3F&text=Solana%20is%20built%20-for%20speed

Wikipedia. (2021, July 20). *Axie Infinity.* Wikipedia. https://en.wikipedia.org/wiki/Axie_Infinity

Williams, S. (2018, January 2). *Cryptocurrencies explained, in plain English.* The Motley Fool; The Motley Fool. https://www.fool.com/investing/2018/01/02/cryptocurrencies-explained-in-plain-english.aspx

Woodley, K. (2021, October 21). Should you buy the ProShares Bitcoin Strategy ETF (BITO)? |

Kiplinger.     *Kiplinger*.     https://www.kiplinger.com/investing/etfs/603621/proshares-bitcoin-strategy-etf-bito

Made in the USA
Middletown, DE
27 September 2023

39550157R00085